SATHER CLASSICAL LECTURES

Volume Twenty-seven

The GREEK ATTITUDE
to Poetry and History

Achilles with his horse Xanthos

Fragment of a kantharos by Nearchos
Athens Acr. 611

The
GREEK ATTITUDE
to Poetry and History

By
A. W. GOMME

UNIVERSITY OF CALIFORNIA PRESS
Berkeley and Los Angeles: 1954

University of California Press
Berkeley and Los Angeles
California

Cambridge University Press
London, England

Printed in the United States of America
By the University of California Printing Department
L. C. Catalog Card No. 54–6471

PREFACE

THIS BOOK is a fragment. The history of ancient Greece and its records do not end with Demosthenes; and the story should have been taken at least to the Roman conquest, that is, should have included Polybios. But there were two reasons, each compelling, why I did not attempt this. First, I did not feel competent to write about the third and second centuries and their historians without a fresh study which the time at my disposal did not allow me. And, secondly, if I had something worth saying at all in these lectures, the subject is not one which could be crowded; it is of the kind which does not admit of summary treatment without losing edge and significance. I have, therefore, in fact stopped at the fourth century; and even so, Xenophon has been, perhaps unfairly, omitted. Indeed, a critic might say that I have only put together some stray remarks about Homer, Aeschylus, Herodotos, Thucydides, and Demosthenes, and the story of their times, remarks that suggested themselves to me first when lecturing on the *Poetics* at Glasgow. My title is, therefore, not only vague, but grandiloquent: it appears to promise too much; but I could not think of a better. I should perhaps explain that, in the title, the words "Poetry and History" form one concept; I am talking of Greek poetry when it concerns itself with a historical subject, and of history when, or if, it is written in a "poetic" manner.

I have left the work substantially as I gave it, in lecture form; there are a few additions, and, especially in chapter iii, one or two learned notes. Doubtless a modern scholar will find in it many indications of "oral presentment."

I am indebted to the following publishers for permission to quote from books issued by them: the Cambridge University Press, from *The Cambridge Ancient History* and from F. M. Cornford, *The Unwritten Philosophy*; the Clarendon Press,

v

Oxford, from Cornford's translation of Plato's *Republic;* and Penguin Books Ltd., from E. V. Rieu's translation of the *Odyssey.*

I must add a quite inadequate word of thanks both to Professor W. H. Alexander for all the trouble he has taken to get my typescript into order, and to Mr. Harold A. Small and his associates of the University of California Press for their unremitting labors in the printing of this book, for saving me from numerous errors, and for the final accuracy and excellence of the presentation.

I have also to thank my colleague at Glasgow, Dr. A. Wasserstein, for reading the proofs.

I cannot conclude without an expression of gratitude both to the University of California for having invited me to give the Sather Lectures and to the very many kind friends I made in Berkeley, who made my stay there both a memorable experience and one so much enjoyed. To leave, even in order to come home, was difficult.   A.W.G.

Glasgow
October, 1952

CONTENTS

BIBLIOGRAPHY OF SHORT TITLES

Alexander, Peter. *A Shakespeare Primer*. London, 1951.

Allen, T. W. *Homer: The Origins and Transmission*. Oxford, 1924.

Bassett, S. E. *The Poetry of Homer*. Sather Lectures XV, 1938.

Beaujon, Edmond. *Acte et passion du héros*. Genève, 1948.

Butcher, S. H. *Aristotle's Theory of Poetry and Fine Art*. 2d ed., London, 1898.

Bywater, Ingram. *Aristotle on the Art of Poetry*. Oxford, 1909.

Calhoun, G. M., in *The American Journal of Philology*, LXI (1940) 257–278.

Carpenter, Rhys. *Folk Tale, Fiction, and Saga in the Homeric Epics*. Sather Lectures XX, 1946.

Collingwood, R. G. *The Idea of History*. Oxford, 1946.

—— *The Principles of Art*. Oxford, 1938.

Cornford, F. M. *The Republic of Plato*, translated. Oxford University Press, 1941.

—— *Thucydides Mythistoricus*. London, 1907.

Finley, J. H. *Thucydides*. Harvard University Press, 1942.

Fyfe, Hamilton. *Aristotle: The Poetics*. Loeb Classical Library, 1927.

Glover, T. R. *Herodotus*. Sather Lectures III, 1924.

Gudeman, Alfred. *Aristoteles: περὶ ποιητικῆς*. Berlin, 1934.

Laistner, M. L. W. *The Greater Roman Historians*. Sather Lectures XXI, 1947.

Mackay, L. A. *The Wrath of Homer*. University of Toronto Press, 1947.

Monro, D. B. *Homer: Iliad*. Oxford, 1906.

Owen, E. T. *The Story of the Iliad*. Toronto, 1947.

Parry, Milman, in *Transactions of the American Philological Association*, LIX (1928) 235–247, and *Harvard Studies in Classical Philology*, XLI (1930) 73–147, XLIII (1932) 1–47.

Ross, W. D. *Aristotle*. London, 1923.

Scott, J. A. *The Unity of Homer*. Sather Lectures I, 1921.

Sheppard, J. T. *The Pattern of the Iliad*. London, 1922.

Stanford, W. B. *The Odyssey of Homer*. 2 vols., London, 1947–1948.

Thibaudet, Albert. *La Campagne avec Thucydide*. Paris, 1922.

Twining, Thomas. *Aristotle's Treatise on Poetry*, translated. London, 1789.

Tyrwhitt, Thomas. *Aristotelis de Poetica liber*. Oxford, 1794.

Vahlen, Johannes. *Beiträge zu Aristoteles Poetik*. Vienna, 1865–1867.

❖ ❖ ❖

In addition to the foregoing I should name three books which are scarcely referred to in the following chapters, to which, nevertheless, I owe much: Paul Mazon's *Introduction à l'Iliade* (Paris, 1943), H. D. F. Kitto's *Greek Tragedy*, 2d ed. (London, 1950), and Jacqueline de Romilly's *Thucydide et l'impérialisme athénien* (Paris, 1947). H. T. Wade-Gery's book, *The Poet of the Iliad* (Cambridge University Press, 1952), did not appear till after my manuscript had been sent to press, or I would have taken much from it.

A.W.G.

I
Homer

WHEN IN chapter 9 of his *Poetics* Aristotle made his famous distinction between poetry and history, that the former was φιλοσοφώτερον καὶ σπουδαιότερον, "something more philosophic and of graver import than the latter," as Bywater translates, we know whom he had immediately in mind, Herodotos and Homer (immediately in mind because, of course, the distinction is a general one and is, or should be, applicable to all others who can truly be called historians or poets); you might, he said, put the work of Herodotos into verse, but it will still remain history of some kind. In thus selecting Herodotos to illustrate his meaning Aristotle showed his good sense, for he is the most Homeric of historians, as the Greeks knew (Longinus 13.3): his range of interest, his language, the very ethos of some of his stories—for example, that of Croesus and Adrestos in book i—come nearer to Homer than do those of any other extant Greek historian. If Herodotos' history is to be so clearly distinguished from Homer's epic, so, *a fortiori*, must that of all the rest. Similarly, in chapter 1 when Aristotle is arguing, more generally, that it is not metrical form that makes the poet, he takes Empedokles as his example of the natural philosopher who wrote in verse but who remained a natural philosopher for all that, not a poet, because his aim, his purpose is a different one; for Empedokles, in his physical writings, was most Homeric in his language, as Aristotle himself recognized in another of his books.[1] Further, in a later chapter, 23, he shows us what kind of difference between poet and historian he is thinking of: not only is the purpose different—for the historian's, like the natural

---

[1] The dialogue περὶ ποιητῶν (fr. 70, Teubner); see Bywater's note on 47b18.

philosopher's, is to instruct and the poet's is to give pleasure—
his special kind of pleasure; but the form, the structure of a
history and of a poem must be quite different. "A history has
to deal, not with one action, but with one period" (59a22), a
poem with a single action—or at least, he adds, it should deal
with a single action, but many poets (he is thinking of epic
poets only) have ignored this salutary doctrine, and Homer, in
this as in other things, shows his easy superiority over others.[2]

The comparison which Aristotle makes is interesting because
both the poet and the historian, Homer and Herodotos, have a
historical theme; for Homer, as for Aristotle, the Trojan War
was a historical event like the Persian Wars for Aeschylus, only
less was known of it. I wish to emphasize this, for we, when
speaking of Homer's predecessors or of his sources, are inclined
to use words like ballad and saga and even folk tale, all of which
suggest fiction and indeed marvelous fiction, legend rather than
historical fact. Rhys Carpenter in his recent Sather lectures
makes the distinction very clearly, but he has a different object
in view from mine, and so uses the words differently. I would
myself prefer "chronicles," as T. W. Allen did,[3] a neutral-
colored word, chronicles which might be in either prose or verse,

---

[2] I cannot agree with Bywater or Hamilton Fyfe, who retain ἱστορίας τὰς συνήθεις of
A⁰ at 59a21–22, reading, the former, ingeniously, καὶ μὴ ὁμοίας ἱστορίας τὰς συνήθεις
θεῖναι, the latter, καὶ μὴ οἵας ἱστορίας τὰς συνήθεις εἶναι, after Vahlen (p. 238). Dacier's
emendation, based on the reading of Riccardianus 46, καὶ μὴ ὁμοίας ἱστορίαις τὰς συν-
θέσεις εἶναι, which is accepted by Gudeman, is much to be preferred. (Riccardianus 46
is independent of A⁰; see Lobel, *Greek MSS of the Poetics*, in *Trans. Bibliogr. Soc.*,
suppl. 9 [Oxford, 1933]). This reading is, for all that Bywater says, less artificial than
his own with its inversion of the order of the terms epic and history; and what excep-
tions to "our usual histories" was Aristotle thinking of? Bywater says: "We have been
told in 51b30 that a poetical subject may sometimes be found in history." True, but
that means that some historical events are amenable to treatment *in the poetic manner*
(as the Persian War by Aeschylus and Phrynichos, if not the Trojan), not that some
histories were composed like poetry. We might indeed have asked why Aristotle said
"some historical events" and not all of them, or nearly all, seeing that the poets were
practically confined to historical subjects (53a18, 54a12).

"Pulcherrimam Dacieri conjecturam in textum admittere non dubitavi; vulgo legitur,
ἱστορίας τὰς συνήθεις, nullo sensu," said Tyrwhitt.

[3] *Origins and Transmission*, pp. 144, 175. I owe much to this valuable book.

but doubtless were in verse and in hexameter verse before
Homer (and doubtless handed down orally, not written), and
which relate, as simply as possible, what happened and how it
happened—in fact, "wie es eigentlich geschehen ist," as Ranke
expressed the ideal of scientific nineteenth-century history; as
Homer or Hesiod would have put it, "as the Muses have told
me," or, to use Aristotle's language in a passage to which I shall
have frequently to refer, not καθόλου, "generically," οἷον ἂν
γένοιτο, "what *would* happen," but τί ἔπραξεν ἢ ἔπαθεν ὁ δεῖνα,
"what so and so did or what happened to him." It matters
nothing whether "what happened" is fairy story, Jack and the
Beanstalk or Odysseus and the Sirens, if the story is told in
this "historical" way; and it matters not a whit that *we* in our
wisdom may doubt the historical truth of the Trojan War,
whether altogether or only in its details; what matters is that
Homer believed it to be historical, and, in our context, that
Aristotle did. For when the latter says that the historian
treats not of a single action, but of a period, he may have had
uppermost in his mind such facts as that no fewer than three
historians began their Ἑλληνικά, *Histories of Greece*, where Thucydides left off—Kratippos, Xenophon, and Theopompos; that
Thucydides, though he only in a digression, in a preliminary
statement, began where Herodotos left off; and that this kind
of beginning was becoming increasingly common in history in
Aristotle's time. The writing consisted of the narrative of events
over so many years of history. More important: the same had
also been the practice of many writers of epic; I should suppose
before Homer, certainly after him. The writers whom Aristotle
here refers to who ignored the rule of unity of subject are not
only those whose *Theseïs* or *Herakleïs* was not constructed at
all like Homer's *Achilleïs*, but more particularly such men as,
conscious that they would be foolish to try to do again what
Homer had already done, as later historians did not wish to
repeat Thucydides' history, wrote the story of the Trojan War
up to the point where Homer began or from the point where he
ended. The structure of an epic or a history might, to Aristotle's

knowledge, be very similar, but only when the former ignored the law of all poetry, namely, that it must treat of one subject and must have a beginning, a middle, and an end. Nothing could be better than the beginning of the *Iliad*, nothing more fitting than its close; but that does not mean, as the lesser *epikoi* supposed, that the former is also a suitable *close*, the latter a suitable beginning, for other poems.[4] Aristotle might have said: even more arbitrary than the author of *Aithiopis*, who literally attached his epic to the last line of the *Iliad*, were the historians who wrote continuations of Thucydides; for Thucydides' ending was quite accidental, determined by his death, so that though it might be thought that Kratippos chose a good year, 394 B.C. (if that was his limit), to end his story, or Xenophon a better one in 362, no one could say that their beginning had any internal logic. Or, rather, we could not say *that* if the aims and therefore the methods of poetry and history were the same; on the contrary, said Aristotle, they were very different, and we must use for them very different criteria: even if it were agreed that some historical theme, as the Persian War or the Peloponnesian War, had a unity which was both εὐσύνοπτον—easily apprehended—and an organic whole, "with a beginning and an end," as Aristotle says that the Trojan War might be said to have (c. 23, 59a31), the purpose of the historian is something quite different from the poet's, and we judge accordingly. For the historian, that is, to begin at the beginning of the Trojan War and finish at its close, or in the middle of the Peloponnesian War because Thucydides stopped there, and continue just to some later date, might be perfectly defensible—but not for the poet.

It should be noted that it does not matter, for the purpose of this particular comparison, how much of the story of the *Iliad* Homer took from the earlier "chronicles." It would, of course,

---

[4] So Vahlen, p. 162. It may be added in passing that the composition of the *Kypria* and the *Aithiopis* presupposes not only the existence of the *Iliad* with at least the beginning and the end as we have it, but that no earlier poems covering the same ground and similarly constructed had survived, on paper or in oral tradition.

be in another way of the greatest interest to know it, just as it is of the greatest interest to observe how much, for some of his plays, Shakespeare was indebted to Plutarch or to Holinshed; but I am concerned with Homer, not with his origins, and, at the moment, whether, for Homer, only the barest outline of the story was historical (only the position of Agamemnon as supreme commander, the presence of Achilles, Diomede, Ajax, Odysseus, and other princes, the deaths of Patroklos and Hektor), or whether he had from his source the story of the quarrel, of the pride of Agamemnon and the different pride of Achilles and the latter's withdrawal from the fight, the friendship between Achilles and Patroklos, makes but little difference—just as it makes little difference that in *The Persians* the account of the battle of Salamis is historically more valuable (and must be consulted by the historian) than the scene of Xerxes' return to Susa. What is important is that everything, whether derived from a supposedly true chronicle or invented by the poet, must be handled in the poet's manner, καθόλου, generically, and not in the historian's who gives an account of what in fact happened. The poet must be "poet of his plot" (*Poetics* 51b30), even when his story is a true one; as Aristotle knew, some historical events were perfectly suitable for poetic treatment.

So far we can go all the way in Aristotle's company, without embarrassment. On the other hand, the poet is in one way or another influenced by historical fact (that is, what he and his audience believe to be historical fact): his attitude to it will affect his story. It is quite true that if he is a true poet he will be composing καθόλου, "generically," telling ὃ γένοιτο ἄν, not ἃ ἐγένετο, what would happen and not just things which did happen; but if in fact these coincide, his narrative will, in some way, be affected. This can be illustrated by the poem I have already mentioned, *The Persians*. Once Aeschylus had decided to include a narrative account of the battle of Salamis in his play, he was restricted in his treatment. Both his audience and he himself knew the main facts, or thought they did; any serious wandering from those facts would strike a false note because it would interrupt the pleasure—the proper, aesthetic pleasure—of the audience; it would for a moment take their minds off the play and make them think of something else, if they thought "it wasn't like that." (Cf. below, p. 64.) Not only that, but, consciously or unconsciously, the poet himself is in such a case inhibited from altering the facts: he could not, for instance, put the battle anywhere but at Salamis. He could concentrate on Salamis, ignore Thermopylai, and refer only to Plataia—though in noble verse—in the prophecy of Darius' ghost; Plataia is not the vital element in his play; but in describing the battle of Salamis he must keep to truth. So with the historic past: in Aristotle's words, Klytaimnestra must be killed by Orestes, Eriphyle by Alkmeon; these are facts that one cannot tamper with (53b23). So Shakespeare can *create* a fine play out of the story of Richard II, but in so doing he was not entirely free. He could not make Richard overthrown by anybody but the future Henry IV.[5] I shall return to Shakespeare later; but meantime how does this affect Homer?

We know that later Greeks believed in the historical truth of the story of the Trojan War, in its main outlines, namely, that it lasted ten years, that such and such persons took part in it, that it ended in the destruction of Troy and the slaughter of its inhabitants, that the Greek heroes, most of them, did not have easy passage home. Thucydides was not given to accepting all the glorified stories of the past that were to be found in Greek poetry, but he accepted the skeletons of these, especially their individual heroes, not only Agamemnon and Helen, but Eurystheus, Atreus, and Chrysippos, Tereus, Prokne and Philomela and Itys, Amphiaraos and Amphilochos, Theseus; it was mainly in his interpretation of past events that he differed from the poets. We can be certain that Homer believed too and, in consequence, that he found the essentials of his story in what I have called the chronicles, what others call the saga or the ballads or folk tales. He found especially the names of individuals and the cities they came from. The *Iliad* is not in all

---

[5] See also below, p. 54, n. 8.

its parts perfect, and there are passages, especially in the *aristeiai* of individual heroes, Agamemnon, Diomede, Menelaos, Hektor, Ajax, and last of all Patroklos and Achilles, which a little try our patience, or tempt the mind to wander, or strain our credulity. In these *aristeiai*, we are told, Homer made up a lot; it was easy to invent proper names,[6] and it was all done to please the princes and nobles as the poet, or the rhapsodes, went from one city of the Greek world to another. Surely not. We might first ask ourselves which cities would be especially interested. Argos in Diomede and also in Agamemnon, but I do not see Sparta taking particular interest in Homer's Menelaos. Did Phthiotis in the eighth century, or in the seventh or sixth, command songs about Achilles from the Ionian poets or *rhapsodoi?* Or Pylos songs about Nestor? Were other cities interested to hear, so briefly, of heroes killed by Hektor? There is one city to which we know the rhapsodes came, by special invitation, in the sixth century, Athens, but alas for this explanation of the long *aristeiai*, there is no "lay" about Menestheus, nor even a digression about Theseus like those which mention Diomede's father Tydeus. Ajax, the near neighbor, is not Athenian in the *Iliad*, even though the text of Homer may derive from the Athenian recension. No; much more probably these many names of men who are killed, who appear in the story only to be killed by one or other of the greater heroes, are from the older chronicles. Some men appear with only their names, some with a descriptive word or two, others with a few lines which bring out some characteristic deed or suffering; Homer has much variety even in these catalogue-like narratives. Look, for example, at the beginning of book vi, (*a*) vv. 29–36, names and nothing more; (*b*) 5–11, just a little more than that: Ajax began the Greek rally

> ἄνδρα βαλὼν ὃς ἄριστος ἐνὶ Θρῄκεσσι τέτυκτο,
> υἱὸν Ἐυσσώρου, Ἀκάμαντ' ἠΰν τε μέγαν τε·

---

[6] Bassett, p. 211. Allen, p. 185, presents what seems to me the correct view. So W. F. Albright, *AJA*, LIV (1950), p. 166, n. 1.

(*c*) 12–19, the attractive sketch of Axylos who lived in Arisbe

ἀφνειὸς βιότοιο, φίλος δ' ἦν ἀνθρώποισι·
πάντας γὰρ φιλέεσκεν ὁδῷ ἔπι οἰκία ναίων·

but his goodness did not save him, for he was killed by Diomede,
he and his charioteer; (*d*) 20–28, ancestry of Aisepos and Pe-
dasos; then, a little later (*e*), the long episode of Diomede and
Glaukos, which has a digression too all of its own, for the epic,
like the long novel, is allowed to introduce an episode for its
own sake, because of its intrinsic interest (provided there is no
inconsistency of thought or feeling with the rest of the story),
and because it gives something of the *past* of the heroes, their
background; it aids the general picture, as Bassett and Professor Mackay have shown.[7] It does not of itself arise from a
previous event or give rise to a following one—especially the
story of Bellerophon does not, which is, in structure, pure digression,—but it does aid the whole story by helping the general
picture. Such episodes "affect not what happens in the story,
but our feelings about what happens in it."[8]

The finest of these pen pictures is that of Lykaon, one of
Priam's sons, who had been once before Achilles' prisoner and
had been ransomed, and twelve days after his return home fell
into the terrible warrior's hands again (xxi 34–53); it leads to
that wonderful short speech in answer to his appeal for mercy
in which Achilles reveals so much of his true character:[9]

Speak not to me of ransom. Before Patroklos' last fatal day, I liked
it better to spare Trojans, and many a one I took alive and sent him
oversea. But now not one shall escape death whom the gods bring
before my spear here in front of Ilion, not one of the Trojans, and
above all none of Priam's sons. You too, my friend, die now. Why
lament? Patroklos is dead, a better man by far than you. Do you not
see me, tall and fair to look on? My father is noble and a goddess is
my mother; yet death and a masterful fate oppress me too. A time

---

[7] Bassett, p. 94; Mackay, pp. 113, 121–122; E. T. Owen, pp. 188–189.
[8] Owen, p. 82.
[9] Sheppard, p. 190; Owen, pp. 208–210.

will come, at dawn or noon or in the evening, when some man in battle will take my life from me, with a spear or by the flight of his arrow.[10]

To resume: these lists of names and the briefly recorded actions or sufferings are there, the great majority of them at least, because they were in the chronicle, much as we find names in Shakespeare's Histories, like the bald list of Bolingbroke's supporters in *Richard II*, or some new names, names only, introduced at the end (II 1.280, V 6 *init.*). Listen to them:

> I have from Porte Le Blanc, a bay
> In Brittany, receiv'd intelligence
> That Henry Duke of Hereford, Rainold Lord Cobham,
> That late broke from the Duke of Exeter,
> His brother, Archbishop late of Canterbury,
> Sir Thomas Erpingham, Sir John Ramston,
> Sir John Norberry, Sir Robert Waterton, and Francis Quoint,
> All these well furnished by the Duke of Britaine,
> With eight tall ships, three thousand men of war,
> Are making hither with all due expedience.
>
> (II 1.280)

Mere names, and not particularly euphonious:[11] there are others introduced at the end of the play, "Salisbury, Spencer, Blunt, and Kent," "Brocas and Sir Bennet Seely," all unimportant, some not mentioned before (V 6). There are the long lists too of French and English dead at Agincourt in *Henry V*.[12] To some degree Homer had difficult, almost intractable material; so had Shakespeare—at least when he was interested. The three parts of *Henry VI* are not greatly inspired; perhaps Shakespeare wrote very little of them; they hardly come to life before scene 5 of

---

[10] Achilles is proud, fiery, fierce, and even savage, but he is never a boaster; he is always conscious of the limitations of mortality, not only when he is with Thetis, or speaking with his horse Xanthos, or in the final scene with Priam, but when he is without mercy for Lykaon, and at his fiercest, after he has killed Hektor.

[11] Sir John Sheppard, who most kindly read the typescript of the first two chapters while he was on a visit to Berkeley at the same time as myself, objected, saying that these names are euphonious.

[12] Act IV, sc. 8, ll. 70 ff. Cf. III 5.39.

the second act of the Third Part. *Henry V* is a success as a play, but not Shakespeare at his greatest. But when he wrote *Richard II*—the vain, weak, and lovable man so unfit to be a king thrust aside by the ruthless Bolingbroke, the man so obviously born to success in this world,—there he found, *in the chronicles*, a story which he knew he could make into a play by transforming the story of what happened to one of "what would happen," without deserting historical truth, or rather (such was Shakespeare's way) partly transforming it, leaving a good deal of incongruous historical residue.

Similarly with Homer, however different the details. He knew, I imagine, from his chronicles these elements: the quarrel, the love of Achilles for Patroklos, the death of Patroklos at Hektor's hands and the death of Hektor, from which he could create his superb story; but that does not mean that he found all his material easy to handle, or that he overcame all his difficulties.[13] No man lives in a vacuum, no man, not even the greatest, is complete master of his circumstances or even of himself, though many of those who pour such scorn on the scholars whom they quaintly dub "unitarians" seem to believe that he can be: at least in saying that Homer was no more the "author" of the *Iliad* than, say, Palgrave was of *The Golden Treasury*, they think they have proved their point when they have shown that there were ballads and stories, epic language and meter, before Homer, that he had his audience and the circumstances of performance to think of, and that through rhapsodes and singers, copyists and editors, his poems were liable to corruption after his death (as much liable, I wonder, as Shakespeare's were in his lifetime?).[14] That is to say, I believe that Homer

---

[13] So Allen, especially p. 169.

[14] It is no less a scholar than Professor Whatmough who likens the *Iliad* to the *Golden Treasury* and to *Hymns Ancient and Modern*, in *AJA* LII (1948), pp. 45–46. Why not to Stobaios? He adds: "That a single editor, or a more or less unitary process of editorship, presumably of great literary talents, enters the picture at some point towards the end of the tradition, (i.e., not later than the sixth century B.C.), seems likely enough." I have noticed that men who deny the poet are generally most sensible of the poetry; and Whatmough ends his article with this sentence about "these immortal epics":

knew from those earlier poems on which he had been brought
up, which he must have known by heart and which must have
influenced him profoundly, as profoundly as the external circumstances of his life influenced him, not only the outline of the
story of Achilles which he was to make his own, but masses of
detail, *historical detail* as he would have thought, much of
which he wanted for his story but perhaps not all of it: he did
not master it all, but treated some not as οἷα ἂν γένοιτο but as
ἃ ἐγένετο. Monro wrote in his introductory note to book xx of
the *Iliad:* "Achilles is burning to avenge his friend; he ought
therefore to seek out Hector and bring his quarrel to a speedy
issue. Instead of this he is drawn away into a slaughter of the
Trojan rank and file, with incidents which occupy two books.
The reason is that the poet has to fill his canvas. The death of
Hector must not stand by itself in the picture, but form the
climax of the last and greatest of the days of battle." This is
well observed, and Bury has spoken of expansion and delayed
action as characteristic of the epic by contrast with the concentration of Greek tragedy.[15] Further, as Sir John Sheppard put
it to me, it enables the poet to show his hero becoming more
brilliant, more terrible, and more savage as the slaughter goes
on. But Homer has not invented (I think) the slaughter of the
rank and file or of most of it, but used that part of the story he
knew for his poetic purpose. We cannot, of course, disentangle
all this material; we cannot be certain about any detail, for it
is now, in the absence of all external evidence, a matter of aesthetic judgment; but I will make two suggestions—or rather
repeat the suggestions of others—where, as it seems to me,
Homer may have been influenced, may have been inhibited, by
what he regarded as the historical fact. They are small matters
in themselves, but may be none the less illuminating for that;
I may be wrong about them, but the suggestions will anyhow

"Their *spoken* descent, through a long line of poets and singers, still rings clear. Who
today ever reads his Homer, even to himself, save aloud, being caught up in the music
of its undying rhythm?" But editors of great literary talents, and processes of editorship, do not leave such an impression on their hearers or readers.

[15] In *CAH* II, p. 499.

illustrate my meaning. You will remember that among other rather odd things about the wall built around the Greek camp, there is reported the wholly irrelevant detail that later the gods destroyed it and left no trace of it behind as soon as it had served its purpose (vii 436–440, xii 3–33). This I suppose, with Rhys Carpenter, to have been in the tradition and to have been kept by Homer because it was in accord with the observed fact; there was, when some of the earlier chronicles were written and when the *Iliad* was written, no trace of any wall in the place where the Greek camp was thought to have been. Similarly in the *Odyssey*, but a more significant case. After Odysseus has been safely landed, still asleep, resting at last, in Ithake by the kindly and efficient Phaeacians, we have the wholly isolated story of the destruction of the Phaeacian ship by Poseidon, which is followed at once by Odysseus' waking (*Od.* xiii 125–187). It is unexpected, it does not "follow from what has gone before," and its ethos is unconnected with the rest of the story; it is isolated. Moreover it gives a bitter edge to Odysseus' imprecation on the Phaeacians when he thinks they have betrayed him (xiii 213), which does not seem to be intentional: "They have brought me to another land though they promised to take me to my own; may Zeus, the god of suppliants, punish them, Zeus who observes what all men do and punishes the sinner"— this just after we have heard that Zeus has allowed Poseidon to punish them for *not* having broken their promise to Odysseus. If the passage about the destruction of the ship is genuine (and I am not quite convinced that it is), it was written just because there was the tradition that Kerkyra was the Phaeacian home and that a certain rock there was the ship turned to stone for all the world to see. It was a concession to fact. I had better add that I do not mean by this that I believe that Homer visited and studied the site of Troy or Kerkyra or Ithake either in spite of a fairly accurate if roseate picture of it (*Od.* iv 605, xiii 242); it suffices if he had heard something about them. He *meant* Troy, that is, the city that was at Hissarlik, and he meant Ithake, I am sure, but that does not guarantee an accurate or personal knowledge. Sophokles meant Lemnos in *Philoctetes*, and Shakespeare certainly meant Rome in *Julius Caesar*.[16]

I believe it is useful to make this comparison, provided that we do not press it too hard, between Homer and Shakespeare and their attitude to the historical chronicle, different as was the genius of the two men and different as were their circumstances. Shakespeare *found* a theme after his own heart in the history of Richard II, Homer in one episode in the Trojan War and again in the Return of Odysseus. Each used a piece of history and converted it into poetry, so did Aeschylus, but each was in some degree bound by the historical fact, both in himself (his own inhibitions) and through what his audience would demand; indeed we should perhaps not separate them, for both poet and audience belonged to their age and were in sympathy one with the other. The poet was however in two things, two essential things, free: he could begin and end where he liked—not arbitrarily, but the *choice* was his; and he could give his own interpretation to the story. To take the first point, the plot, in Aristotle's sense of the word, was the poet's own. "It is clear from the foregoing that the poet is a poet more as the creator of his story than as the creator of his verses, inasmuch as he is a creator by virtue of the mimetic, representational element in his work, and what he represents is action. If he should take a subject from history he is none the less a poet, a creator, for

---

[16] This is why I think the discussion whether Hissarlik *fits* Homer's description (the latest in Rhys Carpenter's *Folk Tale, Fiction, and Saga*) to be largely irrelevant.

I might add, however, that Stanford, in his note on *Odyssey* xiii 242, goes astray when he writes: "Such patriotic descriptions as this would warm the hearts of the Greeks, especially islanders, for the terms would fit almost any small Greek island." There is the considerable difference in rainfall between eastern and western Greece, particularly between the Aegean and the Ionian islands, which affects, in consequence, pasture and woodland; both are Greek, but not alike, and Homer (from what he knew or had heard of the west) was conscious of this:

αἰεὶ δ᾽ ὄμβρος ἔχει τε θαλυῖά τ᾽ ἐέρση
. . . . βούβοτος· ἔστι μὲν ὕλη
παντοίη, ἐν δ᾽ ἀρδμοὶ ἐπηετανοὶ πάρεασι.

A better case for Stanford would be the bay of Phorkys (xiii 96–112), not, it seems, to be found in Ithake, but very true to type; it *might* so easily be there, which is poetic truth.

that; for some historical occurrences may well be of the kind of things that would happen, and it is in that aspect of them that he is their creator."[17] The poet begins where he chooses, he ends where he chooses; he chooses the incidents of the story, including this, excluding that. We should criticize Herodotos if he had passed over the battles of Thermopylai and Plataia and Mykale as lightly as Aeschylus does; we do not criticize the poet even though, as historians, we take account of his narrative of Salamis.

Above all he chooses the beginning and the end. "A beginning," says Aristotle (50b27), "is that which is not itself necessarily after anything else, and which has naturally something else after it; an end is that which is naturally after something itself, either as its necessary or usual consequent, and with nothing else after it."[18] But in history how can an event *not* be "necessarily after something itself," and how *not* "have something else after it," and not simply occurring before and after but explaining or helping to explain the event itself? As R. G. Collingwood has said, the beginning and the end of every historian's work *is* arbitrary in just the way the poet's is not. Thucydides planned to write the history of a war from the first significant incident to its last; that might be sufficiently a unity to be an organic whole. He would begin with the Theban attack on Plataia, but he must first tell in some detail of other fighting which immediately provoked the war and helps to show "the truest cause," and, though much more briefly, the earlier history which tells more of this true cause, as far back at least as the point where Herodotos left off. And why end with the fall of

---

[17] Aristotle does not express himself very clearly in this last sentence, τῶν γὰρ γενομένων ἔνια οὐδὲν κωλύει τοιαῦτα εἶναι οἶα ἂν εἰκὸς γενέσθαι καὶ δυνατὰ γενέσθαι, for he has said just above (51b17), τὰ δὲ γενόμενα φανερὸν ὅτι δυνατά· οὐ γὰρ ἂν ἐγένετο εἰ ἦν ἀδύνατα. I have paraphrased; it is clear that here he means simply that some historical occurrences (as, e.g., the quarrel between Agamemnon and Achilles, or the story of Richard II) are capable of representation as universals, "things which would happen." It seems that the words καὶ δυνατὰ γενέσθαι were not in the Greek MS which was translated into Syriac and thence into Arabic (Gudeman, *ad loc.*) They are certainly better away.

[18] The translation is Bywater's.

Athens? It is dramatically important; but historically? Greek history did not stop there, far from it. And it is not only the obvious fact that life goes on, that there *are* things which happen after the historian's end: to which he might perhaps reply that a man must stop somewhere, and the only question is whether this ending is better, that is, historically more significant, than another? For, what is much more important, the succeeding events help very much to give significance to the end chosen by the historian, to the defeat of Athens in Thucydides' case, so that, paradoxically enough, only a *subsequent* narrative could justify the historian in ending where he did. Grote ended his History of Greece in 301 B.C., after the battle of Ipsos, a suitable close to a long period of Greek history as he understood it, but chosen by him only in the light of his judgment of *subsequent* events and accepted as being suitable by us, his readers, only because we know those subsequent events; it is the later events which give this meaning to the earlier and justify Grote in stopping, since he must stop somewhere, where he did. How much happier is the poet for whom, provided he tells his story right, a tragic death *may* be the end and a happy reunion of young lovers need not be followed by domestic trivialities and babies and all sorts of complications and difficulties. A poem is like the Arabian grammarian's definition of a sentence as "an utterance after which silence seems best."[19] But only provided the poet tells his story in the right way; here Shakespeare in his Histories was, if I may so express myself, up against it. As Professor Alexander, my colleague at Glasgow, has put it in his recent admirable *Shakespeare Primer:* "History may provide the matter for a completely self-contained drama [i.e., one in which the beginning *is* the beginning and the end the end], but then it is no longer history, being detached from the endless chain or interminable web to which history by its nature belongs" (p. 69). And again (p. 71): "Shakespeare, except when his material is particularly favourable, does not in his Histories attempt to secure the unity of action that characterizes the

---

[19] Quoted by Whatmough, *Phoenix* II (1948), p. 66.

Tragedies." Even in *Richard II*, where the material is most favorable, we have, for example, at the end the mention of Henry Prince of Wales, not motived by anything in the play and serving only to point forward to another play or rather series of plays, *Henry IV* and *Henry V*. Professor Alexander points out the difference here between these plays and the Roman, *Coriolanus*, *Caesar*, *Antony and Cleopatra*, also taken from historical sources. There is no true end to the former, not even to *Richard II*, for England goes on; it is, for the moment, history and not poetry. But there is a true end to the Roman plays, for "whatever happens after the death of a Brutus or a Coriolanus is a matter of indifference to the spectator whose interest is consumed in the fire of the individual's fate," just as in the tragedies; and, we may add, it is a matter of indifference to the poet too. To put it in Aristotle's language: Shakespeare in his Histories does not avoid the pitfall of treating a period of time, the reign of a king (or the life of an individual, almost— Prince Henry), as the subject matter of a play; Homer did. Even *Richard II* is, at times, only one of a series of chronicles of England, but, as Aristotle saw so clearly, neither the *Iliad* nor the *Odyssey* is just a section of the story of the Trojan War. This helps one to see as well why Aristotle thought the plot, the story of a poem, the most important thing in it.

There is another aspect of this special excellence of the *Iliad*, that, unlike the other Greek epics and also unlike Shakespeare's Histories, it is self-contained: we must be aware what moral we draw from the story. "In a world of poetic justice a cause so based [the Trojan cause, based on the guilt of Paris] must fail," says Owen, and, further on: "We are made to feel the frivolity of Paris' mind, his indifference to the claims of honour or of other people's sufferings, not for the sake of the moral lesson, but that, realizing the nature of the Trojan cause, we may so far acquiesce in the condemnation of the city." (Pp. 30, 35.) This, of course, would be, precisely, a moral lesson, and one far graver than that drawn from Paris alone. There is something in it: his conduct in the combat with Menelaos and the quickly

following treachery of Pandaros are such "as should oblige the
Greeks" (in Pope's words, true ones, as they so often are) "to
act through the war with that irreconcilable fury which affords
Homer the opportunity for the full fire of his genius." See
Agamemnon's words at iv 164–173, the first two lines of which,
"There shall come a day when strong Ilion will fall, and Priam
and all Priam's people," are echoed with such feeling in Hektor's last words to Andromache, vi 448–449. But it is not essential. Aside from the doubt whether "poetic justice" demands
that all Troy, Hektor, Andromache, Hekabe and Priam, should
be involved in Paris' ruin—Homer is not so simple-minded as
just to contrast virtue and vice,—the story of the *Iliad* is not
that of the fall of the wicked, or of foolish Troy, but of Achilles,
his anger and its consequences, even though we get as well a
picture of the background, of the whole war and the other
heroes, and, in similes, of life in peacetime, and are reminded of
Troy's ultimate fate. Paris does not embody Troy, he is one of
many Trojans.[20] Contrast the historian, if I may anticipate
what I have to say in a later chapter; the fall of proud Athens
is the theme of Thucydides, but that story was to have been
taken to the end, while the *Iliad* did not go on to the fall of
Troy. That was duly noted by Aristotle, and is one of the differences between poetry and history.

Further, the poet gives his own interpretation of the story by
his method of telling it. So, of course, does the historian, any
historian, that is, who is capable of thinking about what he is
relating, which means any historian who is capable of relating.
But again our attitudes to the one and the other differ. We do
our best to understand Aeschylus' interpretation of the Persian
defeat, and, having done so, we accept it as *his* interpretation.
At the most we might criticize a poet for being profound or
trivial—an Aeschylus or a Theognis, as Aristophanes would
have it. The historian's interpretation we also investigate and

[20] Later, p. 77, Owen says that in vii our sympathy remains with Hektor, but against
Paris and so against Troy, as Priam supports Paris. This is not in Homer; he was, in-
stinctively, more subtle than this, and not consciously constructive in this way.

then (perhaps) accept, *simply as his;* but after that we are entitled to ask not simply is it profound or trivial, but is it, however thoughtful, *true,* true to the events he has himself narrated. There are different standards for the poet and the historian.

II

Homer (*Continued*)

IT WILL BE evident that in much that I have said
I agree with Professor Rhys Carpenter's analysis which he gave
in his Sather lectures of 1946, but I am here approaching
Homer from a different direction. Professor Carpenter was, in
large part at least, dissecting the sources of the *Iliad* and the
Odyssey, folk tale and saga and Homer's own "fiction"; I am
concerned only with Homer's treatment of his material, and
especially of that part of it which he regarded as historical. As I
said before, we do not, of course, know just how much he found
in his chronicles: certainly Agamemnon as commander-in-chief
and Achilles and the others as important princes (as well-born
as Agamemnon, his equals in lineage, but, for the purposes of
the war, in some degree subordinate), probably the quarrel, and,
in outline, the characters of Agamemnon, Achilles, and the rest.
What matters is what Homer made of it all.[1] Sometimes Professor Carpenter seems to mean that only what Homer actually
invented by way of incidents or characters can be called his
"fiction"; he suggests, for example, that Eumaios, Melanthios,
and Philoitios in the *Odyssey* are Homer's own, perhaps Pe-
nelope too; this is the fictional element.[2] But though doubtless
Odysseus, both his character and the main theme of his adventure, his long wanderings after the fall of Troy, are from the
"chronicle" (or the folk tale, if you prefer it), none the less
Homer's Odysseus, the figure in the *Odyssey*, is as much his own

---

[1] Carpenter, pp. 71–73, like others, thinks that originally Achilles may have had no
part in the Trojan War; he is a figure apart, by his parentage, by his share in the
fabulous (the arms made by Hephaistos, his horses, etc.), by his loneliness. Perhaps;
but I feel pretty sure that it was not Homer who introduced him into the Greek army
at Troy.
[2] Renata von Scheliha put forward a similar opinion in her *Patroklos* (Basel, 1943).

19

as is Eumaios. So is Telemachos, a character I find of special interest because at times Homer seems to have intended to draw a full-length portrait but not to have carried out the design. At the beginning of the poem, and sometimes elsewhere, he is the tall handsome young prince, who is petulant, somewhat ill-mannered, especially to his mother, weak, and always ready to find fault with others or with circumstances to excuse his weakness—all a natural enough result of his upbringing, and a most interesting study. At other times he is just the conventional young hero. In somewhat similar fashion in the *Iliad* Patroklos is the ordinary hero of the chronicles till after his death, when, in Homer's manner, his gentleness is stressed, his attractive character. (Cf. xvii 670–672, xxi 96, and especially Briseis' lament for him, xix 282–300.)

To return. The whole of the story of Odysseus' wanderings as he tells it in the dining hall of Alkinoös and Arete, with its fairy goddesses, its ogres, and its sirens, may be from folk tale and, for all I know to the contrary, from a folk tale about a bear's son, which is also the origin of *Beowulf*; though why, if it is, it necessarily follows that the Greeks, and even Homer himself, went north to Nordic lands for the story rather than that the author of *Beowulf* went south, as Chaucer did, I do not know. What I am concerned with is, in this context, the use Homer made of it so that it is as much "fiction" in Professor Carpenter's sense as the rest of the poem. The story (I mean here just that account of Odysseus' wanderings up to his arrival in Phaiakia, told by himself) is as well a test of the belief, which I share, that the *Odyssey* is a poem, and a good one—not an anthology. It is in form a digression, and very long—too long, some might think, four whole books, ix–xii, interrupted in the middle self-consciously when Odysseus thinks that the hearers would like a rest (xi 328–384), perhaps a sign that the story would have been too long for the singer in real life. It is full of the fairy-tale element which is absent from the rest of the *Odyssey* as it is, almost entirely, from the *Iliad*. It has its special eccentricity in the absence of Athena, elsewhere the constant companion as well as helper and monitor of Odysseus when, on so many occasions, in such great difficulties, her help was most needed. This absence, you will remember, is rather awkwardly and almost ungraciously noted by Odysseus himself in book xiii (300–302, 314–323). As has been said by more than one scholar, one important episode in it, the descent to Hades, is given a very weak motive because Kirke can and does give Odysseus all the warning and advice that the spirit of Teiresias gives him, and more besides that is of greater help. If any large part of the poem is alien to the rest, whether it be regarded as a later composition inserted into the original or an old independent poem "stitched on" to the straightforward story of Odysseus' return, it would surely be these four books. The story would be intelligible without it; it is digression, and, if you like, too long, a little out of scale. Yet it is, for me at least, impossible to suppose that anyone but Homer wrote books ix–xii, or that he wrote them for any but their present place in the *Odyssey*. To take one part of it first, the Nekyia, the descent into Hades:[3] that is an essential part of the story of such a man as Odysseus, the only mortal (or almost the only one) who had been to the confines of the world of the dead and had returned, as he was the only one (and this is most characteristic of him) who had heard the song of the Sirens and survived. It gives us also that insight into the characters and the fate of other heroes, the onetime companions of Odysseus, which like other digressions in the *Odyssey*, the narratives of Nestor and Menelaos, for example, help to provide a *setting* to the story of Odysseus himself (for he was not the only hero at Troy, nor the only one to have a difficult return home), just as the digressions in the *Iliad* often serve a similar purpose. And how well done are those sketches of Antikleia, Agamemnon, Achilles, and Ajax—Achilles' pride in his son and his bitterness at death, for whom a short and heroic life had not, after all, proved to be what he wanted ("better to be the humblest on earth than the noblest in

---

[3] Except xi 565–627, the appearance of Minos, Orion, Tityos, and others, which is very doubtfully authentic.

Hades"); and Ajax refusing still to talk with the man who had won Achilles' arms from him. And for the digression as a whole, what would the *Odyssey* be like if we did not have the full story of Odysseus' travels and sufferings? We should not know how he came to be alone, nor anything of that physical courage, that endurance and strength of mind, which had carried him through when all his companions had been lost. Odysseus would be so much less a man. More than this: in book xiii, the next book, we have twenty-three lines (70–92) describing the last, the very last, stage of his travels, in the comfortable, smooth-sailing, swift ship of the Phaiakians, from Phaiakia to Ithake.

When the boat was ready, and all the presents and the food and drink safely stowed aboard, and rugs spread in the stern for Odysseus to sleep on, then he himself came on board and lay down in silence, and the rowers went each man to his bench; the ship was cast loose from its moorings, and they swung back and began to strike the water with their oars. Sweet sleep came to Odysseus and closed his eyes, sweet and unwaking sleep, most like to death itself. But the ship, with the stern rising and falling as the great dark wave of the sea seethed in its wake, went swiftly on her way, as swiftly as a team of four horses on the plain that start as one at the touch of the whip and break into their bounding stride to make their course in a moment. So she went safely and surely on; not the falcon, the fastest thing that flies, could have kept her company. Lightly she sped, cutting her way through the waves, carrying a man wise as the gods are wise, who in long years of war on land and wandering over the cruel seas, had suffered much in his heart, but now was lapped in peaceful sleep, forgetful of all he had once endured.[4]

These are lovely lines,

καὶ τῷ νήδυμος ὕπνος ἐπὶ βλεφάροισιν ἔπιπτε,
νήγρετος, ἥδιστος, θανάτῳ ἄγχιστα ἐοικώς.

. . . .

ὃς πρὶν μὲν μάλα πολλὰ πάθ' ἄλγεα ὃν κατὰ θυμόν
ἀνδρῶν τε πτολέμους ἀλεγεινά τε κύματα πείρων·
δὴ τότε γ' ἀτρέμας εὗδε, λελασμένος ὅσσ' ἐπεπόνθει,—

---

[4] This is, with some small modifications, Rieu's translation in the Penguin *Odyssey*.

lovely in themselves, perfect in their context. One line was translated by Virgil, and, by some magic gift, improved:

νήγρετος, ἥδιστος, θανάτῳ ἄγχιστα ἐοικώς
dulcis et alta quies, placidaeque simillima, morti.

But when we look at the passage in the *Aeneid* where that line occurs, we find it is in Virgil's Nekyia, in that grisly story which Deiphobus tells of his mutilation by the wicked Greeks (for to the Romans the enemy was wicked), a repellent story, μιαρόν τι: it is an isolated fine line, not called forth by the context. Homer did not indulge in fine writing; his great passages, such as this from the *Odyssey*, or, perhaps the most moving of all, Achilles' speech to Priam in the last book of the *Iliad*, correspond not to such a passage in Shakespeare, for example, as "This royal throne of kings" and "In such a night as this," but to "How all occasions do inform against me," and Richard II's "Discomfortable cousin"—that is, they are magnificently right in their context. And the context of the *Odyssey* passage is the story of *all* Odysseus' wanderings; it is right because not book v only (his rough passage from Kalypso's isle to Phaiakia and the great storm and shipwreck) but books ix to xii precede, because we have recently heard how

πρὶν μὲν μάλα πολλὰ πάθ' ἄλγεα ὃν κατὰ θυμόν
ἀνδρῶν τε πτολέμους ἀλεγεινά τε κύματα πείρων,

"he had suffered much in his heart in long years of war on land and wandering over the cruel seas." That is not just happy accident, nor the result of a process of editing.

The structure of the *Iliad* is more complex, and, I feel, owing to the larger historical element in it, more interesting. The main lines are indeed, as in most great work, simple, and have been long recognized; perhaps it would be truer to say recognized by some (best by Aristotle), twisted out of all recognition by others. The beginning is perfect, no man has ever begun a story better. The lucidity and directness of the narrative itself, and the way in which the two chief persons in the quarrel, who are to be principals in the whole poem, come to life: their characters, each with his own kind of pride (see for Achilles i 293–303 especially): their relative positions, Agamemnon possessed of the supreme command but only for the occasion, Achilles as well-born as he and a better soldier (xvi 52–54),

> ἀλλὰ τόδ' αἰνὸν ἄχος κραδίην καὶ θυμὸν ἱκάνει,
> ὁππότε δὴ τὸν ὁμοῖον ἀνὴρ ἐθέλῃσιν ἀμέρσαι
> καὶ γέρας ἂψ ἀφελέσθαι, ὅ τε κράτεϊ προβεβήκῃ :

their surroundings, that is, the other princes of the Greek forces, who will play somewhat lesser parts—all this is triumphantly achieved. Briseis, the plaything, the piece of booty destined to be tossed from one prince to the other, is brought to life by a quiet touch in i 348: ἡ δ' ἀέκουσ' ἅμα τοῖσι γυνὴ κίεν, "she went unwillingly with Agamemnon's messengers," as she is also later in ix 341–343 and xix 282 ff.

The middle is, by the nature of things, more difficult to define closely, but its kernel is the Embassy in book ix to the Death of Patroklos in xvi.[5] The Embassy gives the key to the *tragedy* of the *Iliad* (the banquet from which Aeschylus could take a slice); by rejecting Agamemnon's offer Achilles commits the tragic mistake which leads directly to the death of Patroklos and the ruin of his world.[6] It was an offer which he, Achilles, could not but refuse; Agamemnon has not yet been humbled, he has not licked the dust. True, he has not taken Troy without Achilles' help as the dream made him hope he would, and the Greeks have been defeated; but not decisively, and all that Agamemnon has done is to offer great gifts, extravagant gifts, from his own large store, thinking to get out of his difficulties in this easy

---

[5] Beaujon, p. 124, says that the Embassy in ix is just halfway to xviii, the Arming of Achilles, which is the beginning of the end of the Wrath. (Cf. book xiii of the *Odyssey*, halfway through [above, p. 22].) But I doubt if there is any significance in this; see below, p. 26, on book xxiv.

[6] Whether some *fault* in the hero is necessary for tragedy, as Aristotle seems to have held, is debatable (*Hamlet* perhaps proves the contrary; Alexander, pp. 108–113); but Homer's Achilles certainly fits with Aristotle's theory, indeed may have first suggested it.

fashion, like a rich man offering compensation to a poor man he has insulted. It was the best of the examples that taught Aristotle his lesson, not only of the tragic ἁμαρτία, but about necessary or probable consequence of action and character. Achilles' pride *must* revolt at such an offer, though it was proper to offer gifts in such a case, and, as Phoinix says, good manners to accept them. How different is the story of Priam and his gifts in xxiv (147, etc.,) which Achilles does accept. (In a passage of this kind we are often irritated by helpful commentators who bid us "remember that the *ancients* set great store by" this, that, or the other, as though the thing were local and temporary, and only a scholar would understand. On the contrary, Phoinix's urging Achilles to accept is a recognition of good manners which is universal: that Agamemnon's effort at reparation takes the form of gifts, and gifts of a particular kind—seven tripods, ten talents of gold, twenty cauldrons, a dozen horses guaranteed to win the races that they are entered for, and seven young women as clever with their fingers as they are beautiful to look at, of a kind, that is, that would be, some of them, embarrassing to be offered now,—is of minor importance. So is a home universal, and hence we can understand the *Odyssey*, however difficult it may be to follow our guides through αὐλή, λαῦρα, μέγαρον, ὑπερῷον, and the rest, which are only incidental.) With the rejection of Agamemnon's offer, so scornfully and irrevocably—indeed he has hardly listened to it,—Achilles rejects as well the plea of the Greeks in general for his help. "Even if," says Odysseus at the end of his speech, "even if your hatred for the son of Atreus, for him and his gifts, goes deep down into your heart, yet pity the rest of the Achaeans, who are hard pressed in battle, and who will honor you as a god; for certainly great glory would be yours. You would kill Hektor, who now rages among us sure that none of us is now his equal." To that plea at least Achilles might have listened; a little while after, to kill Hektor was the only desire of his heart, but not before his heart had been broken by the death of his friend which his own action had brought about. The later passages in books xi and xvi which have been a stumbling block to so many because Achilles says that Agamemnon has not offered reparation, in fact imply the story of the embassy in book ix, for they would lose so much in significance with that away. Imagine an *Iliad* which went almost directly from the story of the quarrel in book i to book xi, if Achilles' *first* response to what has been happening, the defeat of the Greeks and the onrush of Hektor and his Trojans, were a somewhat offhand "Go, Patroklos, and see if that wounded man over there be not Machaon." In fact, those scholars who would cut out book ix, and with it ii–v and much of vi and vii, from Homer's *Iliad*, and those (generally the same) who would end it at xxii, do not, I believe, really mean what they say; for they know the *Iliad* so well that they do not read it without the books which offend them; the Embassy is there with them as they read the opening of xvi, and they do not close the poem at xxii without consciousness of xxiv.

The end of the *Iliad* has perhaps one flaw, that in the last one hundred and fifty lines Hektor steals the scene from Achilles, the hero of the poem; it is as though Homer had been carried away by his own power of sympathy and had come down to the common level of humanity. Hektor is to the fore somewhat as Dido for a time drives out Aeneas, Falstaff outshines Prince Hal, and as Satan steals the thunder in *Paradise Lost*,[7] though for a different cause. It is Homer's *sympathy*, not only with brave Hektor but with the sufferings of the Trojans. Can one really call it a flaw? For the rest, anyhow, book xxiv gives in generous measure just what is wanted to end the tale. In xxii we were left with the wrath (the subject matter of the whole epic) not only not ended, but at its height, or rather turned to a mad savagery. Achilles' world has been destroyed by the death of Patroklos, destroyed by his own pride and obstinacy, a pride and obstinacy in itself honorable (there is the tragedy), and he has turned his wrath away from Agamemnon to Hektor, the slayer of Patroklos, and now to Hektor's lifeless body. He is

---

[7] Alexander, pp. 72–73.

beside himself, and his noble qualities, not only his accomplish-
ments such as his swiftness of foot, his skill as a soldier, his
boundless courage, but his great courtesy which was shown even
in his wrath or in battle (i 330–336, ix 192 ff., vi 417–420)—all
these qualities are forgotten.[8] There follows the grand funeral
of Patroklos, and then, at the opening of xxiv, there is Achilles,
thinking only of his dead friend, getting no sleep, longing for the
old comradeship and all that they had shared together; then
harnessing his horses once more and dragging Hektor's body
round Patroklos' tomb. Assuredly the story is not yet done.
The wrath is not appeased till old Priam, braving alone the
dangers of a journey to the enemy's camp, going to Achilles'
tent,

ἔτλην δ' οἷ' οὔ πώ τις ἐπιχθόνιος βροτὸς ἄλλος,
ἀνδρὸς παιδοφόνοιο ποτὶ στόμα χεῖρ' ὀρέγεσθαι,

"doing what no mortal man has done before, raising to my lips
the hand of the man who killed my son," begs back Hektor's
body. And it is not only because that is the end of the tale in
the simple sense that the wrath is now over. There is more to a
tragic story than that. The disaster cannot be remedied, the
sorrow is unending, but in some way we are reconciled to it,
reconciled by the beauty of the poetry in which the end is told—
yet not just that, either, for the verse in which the disaster has
been related was fine too,—but by a particular kind of beauty.
When Othello has killed Desdemona and has discovered how
wrong he was, in a sense the story is over, but the poet knew
better than to end his play there; we are reconciled in some
mysterious way to the tragedy by another scene, with the
speech which begins in Shakespeare's incomparable manner:

Soft you: a word or two before you go.

That is what *we* need, a word or two before we go. Sophokles

---

[8] I feel sure that, whatever emendation is to be made in *Poetics* 54b14 (παράδειγμα
σκληρότητος), σκληρότης ("harshness") should be kept. Achilles is, after Patroklos'
death, much more than ὀργίλος, and Aristotle recognized this. See Gudeman's note.

understood that, especially in the ending of *Oedipus Tyrannus*, and Homer too gives it to us in the whole scene between Priam and Achilles (and indeed in the subsequent laments for Hektor), and especially in Achilles' noble speech: "The gods, themselves without sorrow, do not give unmixed good to any man; those are fortunate who receive some good. My father Peleus was honored by them above all, with wealth and with other good things, and with rule over the Myrmidons, and they gave him a goddess for a wife; but they brought evil to him too. No son sits in his home to be his successor; he had but one, me, destined to die young, and I—I do not tend him in his old age, but am here, in Troy, far from my home, bringing sorrow to you and your children"

ἐπεὶ μάλα τηλόθι πάτρης
ἧμαι ἐνὶ Τροίῃ, σέ τε κήδων ἠδὲ σὰ τέκνα.

That is the note on which Homer's tale of pride and anger and warfare ends—Milton's "all passion spent." An epic, says Professor L. Abercrombie, "is not made by piecing together a series of heroic lays, adjusting their discrepancies and making them into a continuous narrative.⁹ There is only one thing which can master the perplexed stuff of epic material into unity; and that is, an ability to see in particular human experience some significant symbolism of man's general destiny. We do not appreciate what Homer did for his time, and is still doing for the world, unless we see the warfare and the adventure as symbols of the primary courage of life. And it is not his morals, but Homer's art that does that for us."¹⁰

Note in passing the difference between the Greek and the Roman. These lines in the *Iliad*'s last book are Virgil's *sunt lacrimae rerum et mentem mortalia tangunt*, the infinite sorrows of human life. The Roman is more obviously literary, the expression is generalized. Homer is generalizing no less (we are here beyond Greek and Trojan), but he embodies the general

---

⁹ Nor, may we add, by pulling an existing epic to pieces.
¹⁰ *The Epic*, quoted by Sheppard at the beginning of his book on the *Iliad*.

in the particular; he does not, so to speak, depart from his story of particular human beings.

I have lingered too long on this aspect of Homer for my particular purpose, but it is difficult not to linger in Homer's company. What at present I intend as my meaning is that all that I have included as the main structure of the poem is clearly Homer's own as the poet of his plot, and not only in its shape but in its ethos. The facts of the quarrel, of the deaths of Patroklos and Hektor, and even of the ransoming of Hektor's body, may have been in the chronicle or whatever was Homer's source, but it is Homer who has given them the shape they have in the *Iliad*, remodeled them, as Shakespeare remodeled Holinshed or Plutarch.[11] Of the embassy in book ix I have no objection to the words "the story of it is no part of the original Achilleïd," but I interpret that to mean that it was not in Homer's source, that it was his *invention* in order to do for the story that he found something of the kind that Shakespeare did for the story of *Hamlet* when he devised the central scene of his play, that of Hamlet discovering the King at prayer and withholding his hand (which, I understand, is not in Shakespeare's source), and the two scenes that come, one before and one after.[12] Further, the scenes in Troy are Homer's own. I have already said, following Bassett and Professor Mackay, that many of the digressions in the *Iliad*, of Nestor particularly, those about Tydeus, with whose example his son Diomede is perhaps too often confronted, and others of an earlier generation or about earlier episodes of the war, taken doubtless from the chronicles, are used by Homer to give a background to the princes, to show the world they lived in; but besides these, Homer gives us in the Trojan scenes (most or all, surely, of his own invention) not only the enemy camp to balance the Greek (for this is war and evenly balanced war), but a picture of family groups such as, owing to the circumstances of the war, he could not give for the Greek side, a picture of how a whole community,

---

[11] T. W. Allen, p. 169.
[12] Alexander, pp. 94–97.

including especially the women and children, is affected by war, a picture done with the variety of which Homer is such a master—the *teichoskopia*, Helen and Paris, Hektor and Andromache, Priam and Hekabe, the laments for Hektor. All this is Homer, and shows both his feeling for balance in his composition and his wide sympathies, his humanity. Observe also how the famous scene between Hektor and Andromache serves, in Andromache's story of how she lost her father and brothers at Achilles' hands when her town was sacked, both to give some of the background of the war and also to bring back to our minds Achilles the redoubtable warrior who, since the end of book i, has been absent from the story. Yet even T. W. Allen, so wise a scholar, could say that Homer must have taken the *teichoskopia* from another and an earlier place in the chronicles because it is so improbable that Priam and Antenor should ask Helen about the identity of Greek princes only in the tenth year of the war, and because in the actual fighting the more eminent Greeks and Trojans generally recognize each other easily enough, as easily as the French and English nobles know each other in *Henry V*. What this does show is that Homer devised the whole scene (primarily to bring *Helen* before us, after all a very important person, the cause of the war) and put it in its proper place, proper not in a chronicle of the Trojan War, but in his own poem. We may feel that probability is a little strained; so it is in Sophokles' *Oedipus;* but we are not much disturbed.

A good deal of the rest of the poem comes from the chronicle, adapted, of course, for his purpose by Homer, who wanted a full canvas and plenty of variety, and who in general has adapted it so well; but there are faults, and these are in the main due, I think, to his being to some degree held fast or inhibited by his historical material or, maybe, sometimes held fast by the exciting nature of a story for its own sake. That particular one of the many "inconsistencies" in Homer which seems to me both significant and difficult to interpret is Diomede's conduct in books v and vi. You will remember that in book vi when he meets Glaukos and asks who he is that dares to advance alone to meet his spear, he adds "unless, of course, you are one of the gods; I would not fight with them. Witness Lykourgos the Thracian; not even he, strong as he was, escaped punishment for his violence against Dionysos." Yet only a hundred lines or so back he has been fighting victoriously against Ares, the god of war himself, and before that, against Aphrodite, and has hesitated only before the terrible words of Apollo (v 440); they are the chief episodes in his *aristeia* in book v, and in line 127 Athena had given him special power to recognize gods when he saw them. He does not now say "I have had enough of fighting against gods," but "it is always foolish"— very much, in fact, what Dione has said to Aphrodite, to console her, about the inevitable punishment that awaits Diomede for fighting against her (a prediction by no means fulfilled). Sheppard compares this restrained conduct of Diomede when he meets Glaukos with his behavior in book iv when Agamemnon, so tactlessly, upbraids him for backwardness in the fight, and he accepts the rebuke; this is intended, says Sheppard, to contrast him with the proud Achilles, who would have fired up at once.[13] I am not sure about this contrast even in iv, for Odysseus and Sthenelos do fire up, and the contrast is with them; and certainly it has not that intention in book vi, for Achilles never fights with the Olympians, nor does any hero of the *Iliad*, Greek or Trojan, except Diomede himself in the fifth book. In fact, when talking with Glaukos, Diomede only repeats the normal Greek view which would equally have been that of Achilles or Agamemnon, Odysseus or Ajax, or Hektor; that is why he does not say "I've had enough of it." The fight with the gods in book v is ignored.

More than this, Diomede's *aristeia* is at an end by line 460 of the fifth book, that is, after the wounding of Aphrodite, in spite of Herodotos (ii 116.3), and there follow three hundred lines of varied fighting of a genuine Homeric character, with many heroes on both sides prominent (note especially 519–520: τοὺς δ' Αἴαντε δύω καὶ Ὀδυσσεὺς καὶ Διομήδης / ὄτρυνον Δαναοὺς πολεμίζε-

---

[13] Sheppard, p. 54. Compare also his article in *JHS* XL (1920), p. 49.

μεν—Diomedes is just one of many), before he again takes first place in his duel with Ares, after which, in book vi, the fight once more becomes general. We realize too that Diomede's *aristeia* has had practically no effect on the course of the battle; it contributes to his own glory but is thereafter also ignored. Further, when in the next book Nestor, urging that defenses be built for the Greek camp and the ships in view of the Trojan threat, begins πολλοὶ γὰρ τεθνᾶσι κάρη κομόωντες 'Αχαιοί, we may, if we like, object that the Greek losses as recorded have not been heavy and have certainly been much lighter than those of the Trojans. Grant all this; we are left facing the fact that it is all essential to the poem. The false dream which Zeus sends to Agamemnon is rightly followed by some Greek success as they go confidently into battle. It is a natural sequence to what has gone before, and, apart from that, it illustrates so well, as Bassett said, Homer's use of the episode. "The Diomedia makes us acquainted with the heroes who captured Troy. More than any other episode it typifies the course of the Trojan War. It also prepares us for the first of the three major peripeteias of the plot, the change from success to failure for the Greek forces, caused by the plan of Zeus. Finally, it is the most interesting of the four battles, if judged purely as an account of the heroic fighting, and without regard to the plot." Homer has taken material from the chronicle and worked it, with easy mastery, into his poem. It was in itself an interesting story, drawn perhaps from more than one source; and if he was not particularly careful to make that part of it where the gods are active (or, rather, where Aphrodite and Ares are active, for Apollo's part is altogether in place) consistent with the rest, that is not surprising when a poet's theme is from history; that is what happened to Shakespeare too.

It has been thought that this particular discrepancy and many others in Homer (some real, some imaginary) are to be explained by the fact that the epic is *oral* poetry, not at first written, and at all times meant to be listened to, not to be read in silence to oneself; not necessarily that different poets and singers have been at work on the whole poem, but the poet concentrates on each episode for its own sake, regardless of consistency; and much valuable work has been done in recent years in the study of oral poetry, especially by Milman Parry.[14] So in the Diomedia, it is said: "There are two themes, one, the hero with miraculous vision, the other, the hero with ordinary vision in battle afraid of the gods. The first is used, completed, and forgotten, and then the second comes in. This is just the sort of thing we found in the oral poetry."[15] I should prefer to put it in a different way: it is the sort of thing you might find in any long poem of the kind that cannot be recited or listened to in a single sitting, or in two or three, but in several, and from which favorite episodes might be more frequently recited than others (after all, Greek tragedy is oral poetry). But having said that, namely, that episodes in a long book may have almost an independent value of their own—and this is as true of the long novel as of Homer,—we have said very little. First because it is the degree and kind of inconsistency which is in question, and this inconsistency in the *aristeia* of Diomede and another which I am about to mention are more disturbing than others. Secondly, because Homer, so preëminently, did not write in episodes, but planned his whole story with, as Aristotle said, a single thread, the wrath of Achilles, running through all his long poem, however much some episodes may be developed for their own sakes. Homer does not, in fact, write in the manner of oral poetry if by this we are to be understood as meaning improvised poetry, handed down from generation to generation of gifted poets and singers, and altered and improved (or spoiled) in the process. His poems are to be distinguished from all such αὐτοσχεδιάσματα, improvisations, again to use Aristotle's word; he is the individual, self-conscious artist; one of a number only as all men are, but as a great artist unique, "a prince, as well as a father, of poetry."

---

[14] See his article in *TAPhA* (above, Bibliography); also Albert E. Lord in the same publication, LXIX (1938), pp. 439–445. Cf. J. A. Scott, *The Unity of Homer*, p. 153.
[15] Lord (see preceding footnote), p. 444.

The second lapse to which I have referred is to me much more disturbing; I have in mind that repetition in book ix of some part, the operative part, if I may say so, of Agamemnon's speech early in book ii advising a departure home. Repetitions as such are, of course, common, part of the convention which Homer adopted from his predecessors or devised or developed for himself;[16] but here is one which, one feels, he would particularly have avoided, for the two occasions are so different. In practically every other case of repetition, the effect is simple and immediately felt by the reader, or listener: compare for example the repetition of Agamemnon's offer to Achilles in book ix. But in book ii Agamemnon, having had the false but most encouraging dream that he will take Troy that very day, decides, quite unexpectedly, with no motive (it is no "probable or necessary sequel" of what went before), to "try it on" with the Greeks, and instead of urging an immediate attack, suggests they all go home; it is, so to speak, a sort of double bluff, Zeus deceiving Agamemnon in one direction, Agamemnon his own troops in the other. And it all comes to nothing; it has no probable sequel. In book ix, on the other hand, the speech is the natural result of *defeat*, *after* the defeat which followed the deceitful but encouraging dream. It is not surprising that in book ii the immediate consequence is almost comic; the Greeks tumble over one another in their eagerness to get to the ships and sail away, and in the end are stayed only by Odysseus, urged to it by Athena. In book ix the speech is followed by profound silence till Diomede protests. I find it hard to believe that both passages

---

[16] Many scholars have noted and attempted to explain the many epic conventions used by Homer, especially the conventional epithets, and recently there was an interesting article by Miss D. H. F. Gray in *CQ* XLI (1947), pp. 109-121, in which she applied the principle of the conventional epithets of persons to things, as the *sea*, the *shield*, and *armor* generally, showing that epithets of the latter which show confusion of types may be due only to combination of types belonging to different periods and indicating changes of fashion. This is true and important; but it is generally forgotten that Homer himself, as the greatest of the *epikoi*, may have invented, and so helped to crystallize, at least some of the epithets, just as, I am sure, he more than any man created, or, if you prefer it, developed the *Kunstsprache* as a whole.

are by Homer, but if either is not by him, it is the earlier, that in book ii.

Sheppard defends the scene;[17] so does E. T. Owen in his sympathetic book, *The Story of the Iliad*.[18] He says that Homer with it "makes us in various ways more fully acquainted with the situation on the Achaean side," before turning to the Trojans in book iii, and that the repetition in book ix brings out well the different feeling of the army on this later occasion. But this is just what is not done; the Greeks, in the rest of book ii, are not at all in a state of panic, but controlled, or more or less controlled, by able princes, and why are they steadier in book ix, after their defeat? Owen says that Agamemnon's misgiving, like his desire to conquer Troy without help from Achilles, is eminently natural. It is; but what matters is that the panic episode is isolated, both in context and spirit, clumsily handled, with the clumsiness felt yet more strongly when we find (if we unfortunately remember) these same lines again, and this time well used. It is weak, as Aristotle notes; but how sensible he is: he does not say that it was put there by an editor of considerable literary talent.[19]

---

[17] Sheppard, p. 27.

[18] See his pp. 17–27, 91–92.

[19] *Poetics* 15, 54b2. See Gudeman. Porphyry seems to have thought that it is Athena's intervention only which Aristotle condemns as mechanical, ἀπὸ μηχανῆς—like the dénouement of *Medea*,—and not a natural consequence of what went before; and Bywater and others follow him. But her intervention is the one natural thing in the whole episode and altogether in line with the usual divine interventions in the *Iliad*. If the text is sound, Aristotle must mean that it is the whole episode which is, not indeed ἀπὸ μηχανῆς, but not "the necessary or probable consequence" either of the previous episode or of Agamemnon's character. This, however, is not very satisfactory, for he goes on at once to discuss the proper use of μηχανή; and I believe Twining was right in adopting Batteux's suggestion that it is an episode from the *Little Iliad* that is criticized, and that we should therefore read ἐν τῇ ⟨μικρᾷ⟩ Ἰλιάδι. Elsewhere in the *Poetics* (59b17) ὁ ἀπόπλους means (as it should) the final departure of the Greeks from Troy, as it does also in Longinus *de Subl.* 15.7, in a reference to Simonides' poem in which the shade of Achilles appeared. There is nothing in the *Iliad* ii passage, either the whole episode or Athena's intervention, which could be described as λύσις μύθου, which is what Aristotle is here discussing. (Vahlen, pp. 163–164, takes ἀπόπλους in 59b7 to mean the pretended departure of the Greek fleet to Tenedos before the episode of the Wooden Horse. This seems less likely.)

I have been discussing these Homeric difficulties because I wish to compare them with the difficulties or inconsistencies we find in Shakespeare's Histories, plays based, like Homer's epic, on what were believed to be historically true chronicles. Let us return to *Richard II* as our example, because in that play Shakespeare is more successful than in any other of his Histories in converting history into poetry, and therefore the "lapses," if I may so call them, are fewer but more noticeable. There is not much even in Shakespeare better than the character of Richard: in his first defiance of rebellion and his subsequent defeat—how in Act IV in his debasement he outshines the ascendant Bolingbroke! But note these curiosities: There is one mention of Woodstock, near the beginning of the play, but we are not told that he is the late Duke of Gloucester, and all the references to Gloucester's death are not to the play, but to the historical event. Toward the end, again, we find a reference to Henry's brother-in-law as though to a character in the play; but who is he? The Earl of Huntingdon, who nowhere else appears. How editors would revel in such things if they occurred in Homer! The one reference to the future Henry V, which I mentioned in my first chapter, carries us only *beyond* the play; contrast in this respect the references to the death of Achilles and the future wanderings of Odysseus;[20] they belong to the characters of Homer's poems, especially to Achilles who chose an early death and fame and for whom honor was essential, while that to the young Prince Hal belongs only to *Henry IV*. On the other hand, the reference to the rule of Aineias' descendants in the Troad[21] *is* simply from the chronicle, outside Homer's story, just as in Shakespeare. Again, Aumerle's plot and his pardon is no part of the organic whole, and Richard's being sent first to the Tower and then to Pomfret is only chronicle. Very characteristic is it that quite by chance, in the few lines on Norfolk's life in exile, we learn that some years have passed since the play opened; they are in the chronicle but

---

[20] E.g., *Iliad* xix 404–423; *Odyssey* xi 119–137.
[21] *Iliad* xx 306–308.

have no significance for the play. Compare again the *Iliad:* by the chronicle Achilles must have been about forty and definitely of the older generation, for his son was old enough to take a chief part in the sack of Troy; but in the *Iliad* he is essentially the young man, destined to die young, with no reference to his son therefore, save once or twice (xix 327, and perhaps xxiv 467), where the boy might be a child of six. More important: Richard's outburst against Gaunt at the end of Act I is not given motive, and Bolingbroke's prosecution of Bushy and Green for their crimes has hardly been justified, and it is the audience who must identify them with the flatterers who have spoilt Richard and by their debased characters ruined him and caused the rift between him and the Queen; for elsewhere we hear of no rift. He is "my sweet Richard" in Act II (the first sympathetic note; he has been scheming and even malicious till then), and she remains a fond wife to the end. In fact we have in Part I of *Henry IV* (V 1.47) an explanation of Richard's difficulties which is more "sensible" than anything in *Richard II*, and, as well, the unkind description of the "ambling King." We can explain all this: Shakespeare was careless of his plots and could choose one altogether incongruous to his characters, as in *Cymbeline*; he had a "practice," as Bernard Shaw puts it, "of recklessly borrowing his stories from contemporary novelists and filling them with his own characters. No plot could restrain Shakespeare's dramatic genius . . . ; but the resulting incongruities are still there."[22] Similarly in his Histories, his English histories, he never got quite clear enough of the chronicles to make a "self-contained drama."

Let us return to the *Iliad* with one or two more cases that seem clearly to belong to Homer's chronicle, from which he has not set himself quite free. The first is a simple one, Priam's many sons and daughters, his wife and concubines (xxiv 493 ff.), an apparently Oriental picture, un-Greek. Yet no Trojan princes, least of all Priam, Hekabe, and their sons, are depicted as *bar-*

---

[22] *Observer* (London), September 29, 1946.

baroi, foreign to Greek ways. In numbers, that is, the family belongs to history, accepted and unadapted by Homer; in character it belongs to the poem which he has created. Second, book xi and Agamemnon's *aristeia*. In spite of the magniloquent introduction (17–46) the *aristeia* itself is weakly motived, and his success is not probable after the story in book ix; and the absence of Hektor from the fighting just at that time is badly designed. He was not there to stop Agamemnon, so Zeus was keeping him away, and as for the message Zeus sends to Hektor, "keep away so long as Agamemnon rages, join in when he is wounded and retreats," that is hardly Hektor's way, and he might have retorted: "I was at the ships this morning; why send me back there only after Agamemnon's *aristeia* is over?" It is stuff from the record again, no better explained than the Duke of York's changing sides to join Bolingbroke in *Richard II*. The whole of book xi, postponing as it does the expected sequence to the Trojan victory in book viii, in form somewhat like books ii–v which postpone the consequences of Zeus' promise to Thetis in book i, is not well designed as part of an organic whole. When therefore I read in Scott's *Unity of Homer* (p. 226), whom Bassett followed (pp. 185–186), that Hektor is unequally treated in the *Iliad*, that he is now the mightiest of the Greeks' opponents, now quite ordinary, that "he is often ignored, though the general, and Sarpedon is the better fighter," I do not agree with their conclusion that Hektor was Homer's own invention, not in his source. On the contrary, the inconsistencies (and they are there) show that Hektor *was* in the chronicle, and that Homer, in adapting it and creating his Hektor, did not completely master his material. Had he invented Hektor he would have known what to do with him and would have done it without hesitation.

There is in Homer no such sharp incongruity between story and character as there is in *Cymbeline*, but very like Shakespeare is the transition from the savagery of vi 55–60 (where Agamemnon stays a temporary temptation to mercy in Menelaos, to which is added the very un-Homeric comment αἴσιμα παρειπών)²³ to the civilized episode of Glaukos and Diomede one hundred lines further on.²⁴ This episode, isolated *as a story* from what has preceded and what follows and so apparently violating a canon of art, yet is justified in the epic because, in giving something of the past of the two princes, it helps, as we have seen, to fill the background; because also it gives variety by making a pause in the fighting, and finally because in its ethos it leads to the episode of Hektor and Andromache—another episode indeed weakly motived (for this was not the moment for Hektor to leave the field in order to take a message into the city in person) but perfect in itself and indispensable to the *story* of the *Iliad*.

It will make for clearness, I believe, if I add a word about another sort of "inconsistency" in Homer, especially as once again it can be compared with similar inconsistency in Shakespeare; I refer now to anachronisms and technical mistakes or confusions. Many have pointed out how difficult it is, for example, to get a clear picture of Homeric armor, still more so of tactics in battle. Every now and again a description suggests a regular formation of troops, infantry, something like the hoplite ranks of classical times. Numbers, that is, the ordinary soldiery in companies or battalions, well ordered, are of importance, but as soon as fighting begins we have only the individual hero and his deeds. He races over the battlefield in his chariot, gets out to fight a duel, is glad to come upon a comrade who is another hero, each of them utterly independent of the troops he is supposed to be commanding; the result of all the fighting

---

²³ Leaf says that Agamemnon's appeal to his brother is to his reason, not to his emotions: obviously not

> ἦ σοι ἄριστα πεποίηται κατὰ οἶκον
> πρὸς Τρώων; τῶν μή τις ὑπεκφύγοι αἰπὺν ὄλεθρον
> χεῖράς θ' ἡμετέρας, μηδ' ὅν τινα γαστέρι μήτηρ
> κοῦρον ἐόντα φέροι, μηδ' ὃς φύγοι, ἀλλ' ἅμα πάντες
> Ἰλίου ἐξαπολοίατ' ἀκήδεστοι καὶ ἄφαντοι.

And the *reasonable*, sensible thing to do was clearly to spare Adrestos and take the large ransom offered. How very different is the αἴσιμα παρειπών (also of Agamemnon to Menelaos) in vii 121.

²⁴ See Owen, p. 57.

hangs on these individual combats.[25] But all this seems easily explicable if we remember that, like Shakespeare, Homer had the historical material of the past as his "source," that manners had changed between the times when those sources were composed and his own, that indeed, if we like, he was ignorant of war and no *historian* of the past, and not concerned to avoid anachronisms and this kind of confusion or inconsistency: the kind of error which, as Aristotle well observed, is concerned with another skill (οἷον τὸ κατ᾽ ἰατρικὴν ἢ ἄλλην τέχνην) and not his own.[26] Unlike the writers of historical novels as we now know them, Homer was not concerned to show his contemporaries what a period strange to them was like. Further, the theme of his story is, like Shakespeare's again (even in his Histories, though they are chronicle plays of England), the actions and sufferings of individuals, not of nations. It is the deeds of Ajax, Diomede, and Achilles, or of Hektor, which matter, just as in Shakespeare's account of the battle of Shrewsbury in the First Part of *Henry IV*, where the numbers on either side are given in their thousands, but the only fighting that we see or hear of is that between Douglas or Hotspur on the one side and Henry or the Princes (or Falstaff) on the other.[27] This is not just due to limitations of the stage and so of different origin from Homer's similar method, but these men, as individuals, are what the play is about.[28]

---

[25] See, e.g., iv 297–300, 446–456, followed by individual fighting, 457–472, et seqq., v 84–94, vi 238–241, xi 284–290, 496–501, xiii 126–135, 307–310. Cf. Mackay, p. 73.

[26] *Poetics* 25, 60b20.

[27] Cf., too, Part 2 of *Henry IV*, II 3.44, Hotspur's widow's bitter complaint about that battle:

> Had my sweet Harry had but half their numbers
> Today might I, hanging on Hotspur's neck,
> Have talked of Monmouth's grave.

[28] This fact, that Homer is concerned with individuals, not families (as also are Archilochos, Alkaios, and Sappho), makes me doubt a common generalization about Greek society before the fifth century, or even after it, namely, that of the solidarity of the family, as expressed, for example, by E. R. Dodds in *The Greeks and the Irrational* (Sather Lectures XXV, 1951), pp. 45–46: "The family was the keystone of the archaic social structure, the first organized unit, the first domain of law. . . . In relation to his father, the son had duties, but no rights; while his father lived, he was a perpetual

Homer belongs to an age much later than that about which he writes, and, as Rhys Carpenter has wisely emphasized, not to those dark ages which, as the labors of archaeologists seem now to have made certain, followed the fall of Mycenae at the end of the twelfth century; he belongs to that great period of activity in travel and discovery when the eastern Aegean had been colonized and trade and colonization in the West were beginning; when new ideas in manufacture and art flourished and when, perhaps, letters were borrowed from the Phoenicians and a true alphabet created. Homer was part of all this, and if we wish to envisage the world in which he lived, the circumstances of his poems, including the *Realien*, we must look to the new contemporary world for them, not to Helladic Mycenae or Tiryns or Troy, for all that the nice discoveries by Professor Wace of houses in Mycenae fit well enough with epic description. I cannot do better than quote Professor Wade-Gery's summary: Homer had his memories from the epic tradition which his fellow craftsmen and their fathers had brought from peninsular Greece across the Aegean. "And I feel sure that almost all which makes the *Iliad* a great poem is the poet's own creation. However close Shakespeare has kept to Plutarch, his Cleopatra is a product of the English Renaissance, not of Hellenistic Egypt; and Homer's Achilles and Hektor, his Priam, Helen and Andromache are products of the eighth century B.C., not of the twelfth."[29]

---

minor. . . . And indeed more than two centuries after Solon the tradition of the family jurisdiction was still so strong that even Plato—who was certainly no admirer of the family—had to give it a place in his legislation (*Laws*, 878DE, 929 A–C)"; and, later: "the relaxation of the family bond," "the growing claim of the individual to personal rights and personal responsibility." There is obviously truth in this, but in the light of all Greek literature I feel that it is the wrong way to express it, that it needs at least considerable qualification; for in the literature the individual, his character and his deeds and sufferings, not the family, is of supreme importance. (*Was* Plato no admirer of the family? The children of the guardians were to regard all persons of the older generation as parents, all contemporaries as brothers and sisters. The guardians must, for the sake of the whole state, be denied family life; but they had also to be denied poetry, which Plato greatly admired.)

[29] *AJA* LII (1948), p. 116. Nor of the seventh century, where Rhys Carpenter would put Homer. I do not for a moment believe that we can precisely date the *Iliad* and the

I should like to end my remarks on Homer by saying something about his impartiality—not perhaps a very good word to use of a poet, and I use it for want of a better; but I propose to say something later of the impartiality of Herodotos and Thucydides, to whose work, since it is history, the word is appropriate, and I am still thinking of Homer's *historical* theme. I shall say what I have to say on this topic about each writer in turn and explain my whole intention at the end.

I begin with a sentence from the late Professor Bassett's Sather lectures (XX, p. 218), a sentence which I do not know how he, who understood so much in Homer, came to write: "That leaders of the enemy [Glaukos and Sarpedon] should be thus ennobled is strange in a poem so national in character." What does this mean? Why Glaukos and Sarpedon? We can think of other "enemies" thus ennobled, *Hektor*, Andromache, Priam, Hekabe, and of course lesser Trojans, such as Aineias and Antenor, treated with the same sort of respect that Greek heroes get. Put in its right perspective this talk of "enemies" and "nationalism" is surely irrelevant to Homer. As reasonably we might express surprise that Helen, the cause of all the woes of the Greeks and the Trojans, is not vilified.

Yet Homer was human and there are weaknesses in him too.

Odyssey, as he does, the one to within twenty years or so of 675 B.C., the other to 625, on the basis of our knowledge of conditions in the eastern and western Mediterranean in the seventh century; see the illuminating papers of Hanfmann and Albright in *AJA* LII (1948), pp. 135-195, and LIV (1950), pp. 162-176, which suggest very different conclusions; also Dunbabin's *The Western Greeks*, especially the convincing discussion on the chronology of the Greek foundations, pp. 435-471, which shows that by 700 B.C. at least, most probably half a century earlier, Sicily and the southern and western coasts of Italy were known to the eastern Greeks. Homer should not be put later than the second half of the eighth century; the earliest of the other Greek poets, Hesiod probably, Tyrtaios, Archilochos, Alkman, Sappho, all knew his work. Albright would put him a good deal earlier, in the first half of the tenth century, because he knows nothing of Phoenician settlement in the west, which was *ca.* 950 B.C.; but ignorance, or silence, is by no means a convincing argument. Besides, sometimes poets keep to the facts of ancient history; in *Cymbeline* Shakespeare was careful not to call the British English.

It is worth noting as well that the songs which the colonizers brought from peninsular Greece to the islands and the Ionian coast did not, apparently, include laments for the destruction of the great Achaean cities—no memories as, further north, of Kossovo and Mohacs Field.

In book iv, after lordly Agamemnon's ἐπιπώλησις, his stately survey of his troops, when he has rebuked the Greek leaders for their pusillanimity and encouraged them to stand their ground, we have one of those pictures of the Greeks as a compact, orderly, hoplite army which I mentioned above; then, by contrast, the Trojans (vv. 422–438):

Thus in closed ranks the regiments of the Greeks moved forward to battle, ceaselessly; each of the leaders gave orders to his men, and they marched in silence. You would say that there was no voice heard in all that host as they watched in silence for their commands, and on them all their armor shone in varied brightness rank upon rank. The Trojans, like the innumerable sheep of some rich man who wait in a fold to be milked, bleating always as they listen to the cries of their lambs—just such a noise arose in the widespread army of the Trojans. For there was no one command, no single voice, but all tongues were mixed in their ranks, and the men had many names.

A strange picture of the Trojan army (like that of Xerxes later in Herodotos, but unlike Aeschylus' picture in the *Persai*, 374–383), almost isolated in the *Iliad*, though the Trojans in council are similarly called a chattering group (vii 346); it is here apparently intended simply to provide a contrast to the well-ordered, quiet ranks of the Greeks. Even when in book ii the Greeks had run to their ships, every man anxious to get home, "calling upon each other to get hold of the ships and put to sea, and a great din rose to the skies" (vv. 151–153), they are not so unflatteringly described as the Trojans.

Another instance is the treachery of Pandaros, occurring so soon after the poltroonery of Paris; it is the sort of thing that is ascribed to an enemy. And yet again: we know how often the gods, one or another of them, helping their favorite heroes, are said to direct the spear thrown at the enemy, or divert the one thrown by the enemy, an account of the relation between divine and human beings which we easily accept and which does not, generally, in any way detract from the courage or the skill of the princes, any more than the message of Iris and the help of Hermes detract from old Priam's courage in book xxiv. But every now and again we find that the gods' intervention does lessen the merit of the Trojans. Thus in book viii (130–136), when in fact Hektor is more than holding his own, and Diomede has just rescued Nestor and is beginning to rage among the Trojan ranks,

then would disaster have befallen the Trojans and irremediable deeds have been done and they would have been herded like sheep within the walls of Ilion had not Zeus perceived it and sent a great thunderbolt to fall before Diomede's chariot,

so that he turns back and Hektor presses on in triumph. Later, Hektor, who has been said by Agamemnon (vii 109–121) to be the superior of all the Greeks except Achilles, is pictured as avoiding, even in his hour of victory, combat with Ajax (xi 542). Generally in his *aristeia* Hektor gets far more help from Apollo than any Greek gets from Athena or Hera, and the Greek defeat is thus, after a manner, explained away, particularly in the most important episode of all, the death of Patroklos (xvi 712 ff.). For, though Hektor seeks him out, ignoring other Greeks, yet it is Apollo who first disarms Patroklos, then another Trojan, Euphorbos, wounds him from behind, not staying to fight further, unarmed though his enemy was. Patroklos begins to retreat, and then Hektor, observing him wounded and retiring, attacks and kills him; and the dying Patroklos taunts him with just that.

Owen indeed maintains that Homer had a purpose in this, that he "piled up point after point in his description of the circumstances of Patroklos' death so that even the least imaginative reader must burn with indignation at the way it is accomplished. This is what Homer wants, for he is motivating the terrific fury and grief of Achilles. We can sympathize much better with the extravagance of his feelings because we too have resented the manner of his slaying." But this, the *manner* of Patroklos' death, is not given as the cause of Achilles' raging, and, in any case, the explanation does not do away with the objection that it has something of τὸ μιαρόν, what is repellent, in it and is quite inconsistent with Hektor's character elsewhere in the poem; he is not only chivalrous, but, as the equal or superior of all Greek heroes except Achilles, does not need all that aid from Apollo and certainly not the unpleasant assistance of Euphorbos. We should not deny that this is Homer playing to the groundlings (the groundling in all of us), feeding the easiest of nationalist sentiment. After all, he does it very seldom, nothing like as much as Shakespeare, in *Henry V*, for example, in which, apart from the artistic sin, even the patriotic appeal would be more effective without it; for what is English Harry's victory worth, if the French are all to be shown as ignorant and conceited popinjays? In Homer there is so little of this that we do not comment on the humanity which he shows elsewhere; it is what he has taught us to expect. We do not feel surprise that in him the enemy is not "wicked," nor Helen, though I read recently this as a summary of her part in Homer: "Helen had no choice but to be a byword for adultery in after ages"—just as though *Iliad* iii and xxiv had never been written. Leaf says in his comment on the disarming of Patroklos by Apollo that we would be wrong to trust to our own idea of chivalry. How true; but we are right in trusting to Homer's, who elsewhere shows a very different Hektor, and actually here Patroklos' taunt makes clear the feeling that is certainly not to be found only at the present day. What a wide gulf there is between these insults that pass between Hektor and the dying Patroklos and Hektor's speech to Andromache in book vi, in which he foretells his own approaching doom, the fall of Troy, and his wife's captivity:

Well I know in my heart that the day will come when great Ilion will fall, and Priam and all Priam's people. Yet not for all the Trojans have I such grief, not for Hekabe herself, or Priam, or my brothers, many and brave as they are, whom the enemy will strike to the ground, as for you, dragged off weeping by some Achaean warrior, deprived of your freedom. There in Argos will you be working at some other woman's loom, or bringing water from a well in Messeis or Hypereia; hard it will be for you, but harsh necessity will be on you.

"This is the wife of Hektor," someone will say as she sees your tears, "the bravest of all the horse-taming Trojans when the war was on around Troy." That is what they will say; you will feel a new grief at the loss of the man who should have kept you free. May the earth lie heavy on my dead body before I hear your cries as they lead you away from here. (447–465)

This is the true Homer, as we express it, though that does not prove that the same man did not write both passages. In the wake of Leaf and in a similar vein Bassett wrote that *for Homer* Achilles could do no wrong, the rejection of the embassy in book ix being a mere error of judgment, and "it was a duty and act of piety" in him to outrage Hektor's body (pp. 203–204). What then did Homer mean by giving to the dying Hektor the plea to Achilles to surrender his body to his kin in Troy, and to Achilles a savage refusal? Why do the gods, during all the days that Achilles is outraging the body, keep it unsullied and free from decay? If Achilles is all white, without blame, "a model for all" (pp. 188–189), there would be no tragedy in the *Iliad*; if he merely made a mistake, a miscalculation of the odds which unfortunately ended in his friend's death, and if he thereafter behaved in every way as a brave and a good man should, there is pathos there but not tragedy. On the contrary, his fault was a moral one; he was responsible for the disaster to his own life and to that of others. The fault had its source in noble instincts, but that makes it the more tragic. That is what Aristotle meant in the passage Bassett refers to in defense of his own view (13, 53a14): "The change in the hero's fortune must be from happiness to misery, and the cause of it must lie not in any depravity, but in some great error on his part" μὴ διὰ μοχθηρίαν, ἀλλὰ δι' ἁμαρτίαν μεγάλην. Bassett does confuse tragedy with the pathetic, as when he says (p. 235) that there were two tragedies to be made out of the *Iliad*, not one, as Aristotle said, namely, that of Achilles and that of Hektor. For Hektor is not a tragic figure any more than he is the hero of the poem; he is a man with a greater claim on our affections than Achilles (Bassett, pp. 188–189), but tragedy demands more from us than sympathy. Othello is the tragic figure, not Desdemona; Macbeth and Lady Macbeth, not Duncan; Medea, not her children, since young children, having no power of decision (no προαίρεσις), cannot be tragic, only pathetic. Tragic figures do not only suffer; by their own actions, by their own choice, which is not due to *depravity* of character, they are the cause of suffering to themselves and to others.

Imagine another poet, a good poet with a descriptive power equal to Homer's, but a lesser man for all that, taking the story of Achilles from the chronicle and deciding to make his poem one about the peerless young warrior who kills his chief enemy Hektor, but, as he and we know, is destined to die young, and in the end is killed by Paris, the least man among the Trojans. That could have been a very fine and affecting story; but it would not be tragedy. Achilles would not in this case have caused the suffering, his own and that of others; it would not be *his* doing, the result of a fatal, though not base, streak in his character which made his choice inevitable. Homer knew better: instead of Achilles' death, we have the story of the wrath, and Homer's Achilles is no "model for all" to follow.

I have passed from the subject of what I may call historical impartiality in Homer (between Greeks and Trojans) into artistic impartiality (no mere contest between black and white), though in a poet with a historical theme the two cannot be separated; but I will return to the former with another quotation before I close. I read the following in a recent review of Haarhoff's new book on Virgil: "Even in the underworld the enmity between Greeks and Romans is not forgotten, and Virgil has no tears to shed over the destruction of the famous cities of Greece. There were limits to Virgil's sympathies."[30] How strangely that reads to one fresh from Homer. "Virgil has no tears for Greek cities." One cannot *read* that speech of Hektor's to Andromache without tears, and the end of the whole poem is a lament for Hektor and for Troy.

I may appear to have got a little far from my theme of poetry

---

[30] M. L. Clarke, in *CR* LXIV (1950), p. 156.

and history and Aristotle's view that poetry is the more philo-sophic and the more profound of the two, but I hope that the logic of this procedure will become clearer when I come to the historians. Before I do that, however, it has seemed to me, in the course of preparing these lectures, necessary to get a more precise idea of what Aristotle meant in certain passages in the *Poetics*, by μίμησις, for example, the theory of art as "imitation," and whom he had in mind when he spoke of history and comedy. I found that I disagreed with some learned editors in certain matters which directly or indirectly concerned me. That is the foundation of the next chapter.

III

Some Problems in
Aristotle's "Poetics"

THAT THERE IS a wide distinction between poet and historian, even when like Aeschylus and Herodotos they are dealing with the same theme, that they have different aims and are working in different worlds, we accept, and it is one of the major merits of the *Poetics* that it makes this distinction so clearly. Aristotle goes on from this point to say that poetry is something more philosophic and of graver import than history, φιλοσοφώτερον καὶ σπουδαιότερον, and I wish to discuss the meaning of this. But before I set about doing so, it will be well, I think, to clear away certain confusions, as I regard them, about Aristotle's attitude, as expressed in the *Poetics*, to poetry and to art generally.

First: should art be didactic, using the word "didactic" in its widest sense? should art *aim* at making men better, whether with a cloistered or a political virtue, better men or better citizens, using also the word "better" in the widest sense, to include, e.g., the development of greater sensitivity of eye and ear? Not *does* it make men better, but is that its purpose? It is still sometimes said that Aristotle followed the common Greek view, that it is, but I agree altogether with Bywater that, on the contrary, his view is that the purpose of poetry, and of art generally, is to give pleasure, a peculiar kind of pleasure maybe, each kind of poetry giving its own proper pleasure; he says so several times, quite clearly,[1] and I need only refer specifically to the sentence in c. 14,[2] "Those who make use of the Spectacle"

[1] 48b18; 50a33; 51b26; 60a17; 62a16, stated generally: more particularly in 53a36; 59a21; 62b1, 13.
[2] 53b11–12.

49

(the purely spectacular element in any play seen upon the stage) "to put before us that which is merely monstrous and not productive of fear, are wholly out of touch with Tragedy; not every kind of pleasure should be required of a tragedy, but only its proper pleasure. The tragic pleasure is that of pity and fear";[3] and I may mention again the distinction which Aristotle draws between the poet and the man who *teaches* a theory of medicine or physics in a metrical form (47b18). But I would go further and say that this would also be the view of all intelligent Greeks who had interested themselves in the question, Aristophanes, for instance. There were ignorant Greeks (ignorant in this one sphere of knowledge, I mean) who supposed that Homer made it his business not only to make men better, but to teach them theology, military tactics, and much else besides; there were many who thought it the main purpose of poetry, especially of tragedy because it was a public spectacle, to make men better. Aristophanes makes fun of these; Plato takes them seriously, or pretends to do so. The existence of such types does not differentiate the Greeks from other men; in later times Shelley, Byron, Swinburne, have been both defended and attacked for the immorality of their *doctrines*, modern poetry and music for its *effect on the mind*. What, it will be objected, even if we allow that Aristophanes was not always as solemn as an owl, what of Plato? and what of the theory of purgation of pity and fear? Surely that is a didactic theory of some kind.

The answer is that Plato was not writing about the theory of poetry, or of art in general, but about politics, politics in the wide Greek sense, the life of men in a community. If your main concern, at the time, is with politics, and if you are convinced, as Plato was, that it is the business of the community, through its laws or its governors, however these are chosen, to do its best to improve the moral and intellectual standards, as we should say, of the citizens, then, of course, you must face the question whether the existing music, poetry, and art that men are listening to or seeing with their eyes does good or harm; for whether

---

[3] Bywater's translation.

we like it or not, art will, if it has any kind of merit, do one or the other. We may disagree with Plato when he says that Greek art and poetry did more harm than good, and, even if we admitted that they were doing harm, we may disagree with him that the proper remedy was their suppression, or rather their regulation, by the government; but we cannot deny that the political or, as we should probably call it, the social problem is there. If a man were today as sincerely, as intelligently, and as sensitively concerned with the state of society as Plato was in the fourth century B.c., he could not pretend that the music heard and the pictures seen by all or most citizens are a matter of indifference; only a man blind and deaf could think that we could listen, day after day, to jazz music or to the sentimental musical comedy of thirty or forty years back, or go as frequently as we do to the cinema, without being, in some way, affected by it for good or evil. But to admit that is not to say that the *purpose* of the cinema or of musical comedy is or ought to be anything but the giving of pleasure, its own proper pleasure; it only means that the *political* question is: does the pleasure do harm or good, and would it do harm or good if the community tried to control it? If then you are writing a book about the art of the cinema, you are concerned only with its proper function, the way it does its duty, so to speak, perhaps also with its history and how it reached fruition, its τέλος.[4] That is what Aristotle is, almost wholly, concerned with. If he has a didactic or practical purpose at all in the *Poetics*, it is quite a different one from Plato's in the *Republic*; it is to help others in the difficult art of writing a tragedy or an epic. True, he makes a defense of tragedy, a social defense, the famous one that it causes a purge of pity and fear; that *is* his argument against Plato, that Plato was wrong in his initial assumption that tragedy did harm. But in the *Poetics*, that is only by the way; it is not his proper theme. Plato loomed so large in the learned world of the mid-fourth century, and especially for Aristotle, that his doctrine, though a political and not an aesthetic one, could not be just passed over;

---

[4] See Kitto's introduction in his *Greek Tragedy* (London, 2d ed., 1950).

this does not mean that Aristotle agreed with the didactic theory of art. That is why I emphasized that particular sentence in which he talks of the pleasure of tragedy, its οἰκεία ἡδονή : τὴν ἀπὸ ἐλέου καὶ φόβου διὰ μιμήσεως δεῖ ἡδονὴν παρασκευάζειν τὸν ποιητήν, "the tragic pleasure is that of pity and fear, and the poet has to produce it by μίμησις, representation, in some way, of human life"—the *pleasure*, not the social or moral benefits, which comes from tragedy. It is wrong to say that this purgation of certain emotions is, for Aristotle, the end, the purpose, of tragedy; its end is its own proper pleasure.[5] The theory of purgation in the *Poetics* is only an incidental social defense of it. Hence we are not obliged to suppose that there was a similar social defense of comedy in the lost second book of the *Poetics* because Plato banned comedy as well as tragedy.[6]

A frivolous example will perhaps make my argument clearer. Suppose that Aristotle were writing a book about gambling. He would have defined its purpose, perhaps, as "a pleasurable way of losing money," its οἰκεία ἡδονή, the pleasure proper to it, "for it is clear," he would doubtless have added, "that other ways of losing money are unpleasant rather." He would have analyzed its means and its methods: whether one gambled at horse racing, the casino, in a state lottery, or what not; if on horses, whether by street-corner betting or on the course, and if on the course, whether with bookmakers or the totalizator. He would have set apart gambling on the stock exchange on the ground that the purpose of this form of betting was to *make* money. He would

---

[5] Bywater is misleading on this, pp. 150 (note on 49b24), 151 *ad fin.*, and 155–156. He is more accurate on p. 161, where he distinguishes between the functions of the poet and the statesman.

[6] In his paper in *Wiener Sitzber.* LXXVII (1874), pp. 293–298 (= *Ges. Philol. Schr.* I, p. 230), Vahlen argued that the fuller discussion of the κάθαρσις of tragedy and comedy, as promised in *Pol.* viii 7 and summarized by Proklos, came in the second book of the *Poetics*, after the account of comedy, and wrote as follows: "Nach der theoretischen Abhandlung beider dramatischen Gattungen konnte aber füglich erst die Frage nach der Nützlichkeit beider für das öffentliche Leben aufgeworfen werden, deren Entscheidung nothwendig durch die Prüfung ihrer Wirkung auf den Zuschauer bedingt war." This may be a correct conclusion; but it assumes that a discussion of the problem of the "usefulness" of tragedy and comedy was part of the design of the *Poetics*, and this, if we are to judge by what we have of the book, is improbable.

have added a little about the history of gambling and given some advice on how to bet most wisely—that is, of course, how to get most pleasure out of losing money. Now if Plato had roundly condemned gambling and driven it from his republic, as he probably would have done had it been a habit with the Greeks to bet at their national games, on the ground that it stimulated evil appetites in the soul, love of money and of getting it without deserving it, Aristotle might very well have put in a defense that periodic gambling, as in a modern state lottery, does good by purging us of those appetites which we all have in some degree. This would not mean that his *purpose*, or one of his purposes, in writing the book was a political defense of gambling, only that Plato's views on any matter were not to be ignored. And *we* might agree with the political views about it of either Plato or Aristotle without having different views about the nature and purpose of gambling, and without supposing that Plato and Aristotle had.

Secondly, Bywater, in his dry way, refused to say anything about Aristotle's attitude to art in general and repudiated the title of Butcher's book, *Aristotle's Theory of Poetry and Fine Art*. I think that Butcher here was in the right, or more nearly in the right. Aristotle's frequent references to sculpture and painting, his use of μίμησις as freely when writing about poetry as about the visual arts, including dancing (e.g., 48a5), show that he thought they had enough in common to make possible some useful generalizations that would cover both—that, rightly or wrongly, he had a theory of poetry and fine art. This leads me directly to my third preliminary point; what did Aristotle mean or imply by the word μίμησις, which Bywater persisted so firmly in translating "imitation"? Bywater leaves us in no doubt about what *he* thought Aristotle meant. For example, on the meaning of the word ποιητής itself he says (on 47b22): "The poet was distinguished from the historian or chronicler by the fact that he was so constantly dealing with a remote or legendary past, in the treatment of which there was ample room for play of imagination. All the great poetical subjects are classed by Plato under the general head of 'myths' or fictions . . . ; and it was an understood thing that a free use of fiction was one of the privileges of the poet: thus Solon, fr. 29, πολλὰ ψεύδονται ἀοιδοί ['What a lot of lies the poets tell.'] . . . This recognition of an element of fiction in poetry is perhaps the nearest approach the ancients make to our idea of 'poetic creation.' The ordinary conception in antiquity of the poet was that he was, just like the painter, an imitator, and that his work was not so much a creation as a copy, more or less faithful, of something already existing in legend or life."

This is in manifest contradiction to Aristotle's own words, employed more than once, that painters and poets must necessarily "imitate" men (to use Bywater's translation of μίμησις for the moment) as better or worse than they are, or just like them; and that the art that makes them "better" is the highest and most worthy of consideration. (For the meaning of "better" see below, p. 65.) How can an "imitation" which is deliberately designed to show men as "better" or "worse" than they are be said to be "a copy more or less faithful of something already existing"? Such a description might, very superficially, apply to Menander, who portrayed men "as they are," but not to those whom Aristotle most admired and had always in mind, Homer, Sophokles, Polygnotos. Is Homer's Achilles or Sophokles' Oedipus a more or less faithful copy of some existing individual in legend or in life? And could Aristotle have thought that they were and yet have written in the way he has? This Butcher saw clearly;[7] Bywater was perverse. The very word ποιεῖν, used of the visual as well as of the oral arts, means "to create."[8]

---

[7] Pp. 116, 121 ff. Perhaps the sentence which most clearly shows how wrong Bywater was to limit the meaning of μίμησις to photographic copying is that on "mistakes" by a poet—do they touch the essentials of his art or only some accident of it? ἔλαττον γάρ, εἰ μὴ ᾔδει ὅτι ἔλαφος θήλεια κέρατα οὐκ ἔχοι, ἢ εἰ ἀ μ ι μ ή τ ω s ἔγραψεν (60b32), where ἀμιμήτως means "in a manner unsuitable to art," but Bywater translates "unrecognizably," with a reference to 48b15 (below, p. 64).

[8] Note the story told by Ion that Sophokles said that if a painter painted Apollo's hair golden, and not black, he would make a worse picture (Athen. xiii 603E). A wise

We may add that dancing, by a chorus in tragedy or comedy, or in the dithyramb, was also μίμησις; of what in life was that formal and conventional movement, those "tunes," a more or less faithful copy, in the restricted sense? Besides, the poet, for Aristotle, was not distinguished from the historian or chronicler by the fact that he was dealing with a remote or legendary past; on the contrary he tells us clearly that the lesser ἐπικοί, epic poets who did not possess Homer's instinctive understanding of the nature of poetry, were just like chroniclers, as we have seen, and the fact that they wrote in the same meter and were dealing with the same remote past does not give them a title to the name of poet. Or, to put it positively, when the true poet takes a *historical* theme, "he is none the less a poet," for he treats it in a poetic way, as "something which would happen," not as "a record of something which did happen"; he creates his own μῦθος, "story," just as certainly as if he were making up his own plot. This is, as we saw, further evidence that for Aristotle the μῦθος or structure, the plot of a tragedy or epic, is the

remark; gold paint because more expensive is more grandiloquent and would have a wider popular appeal; it is "better than ourselves," more obviously than black hair; further, and this is perhaps most important, it would be more "like the original," the Ἀπόλλων χρυσοκόμας of the tradition. All this did not make Sophokles, who "portrayed men as they ought to be," believe that the picture would be better for the gold.

In 54a24 Aristotle mentions τὸ ὅμοιον among the proper qualities to be found in a tragic character; this Butcher, Bywater, and Gudeman agree means "likeness to the original in legend or history." So Ross, p. 288. A case in point would be, presumably, that Achilles in a tragedy must be not only a prince but a proud prince, a great warrior, etc. This may be right, though the contrasting treatment of Odysseus in different tragedies should be remembered; but I believe that ὅμοιος there means "like ourselves," as in 53a5–10—not wholly good, which is clearly what is implied by ἐπιεικής in 52b34, any more than wholly bad. Thus ὥσπερ εἴρηται will then take its natural meaning, "as has been said above," not "in our sense of the term" (referring only to ἅρμοττον or χρηστὸν καὶ ἅρμοττον). Bywater quotes Aristotle's example of the portrait painter just below to confirm his interpretation, καὶ γὰρ ἐκεῖνοι ἀποδιδόντες τὴν ἰδίαν μορφήν, ὁμοίους ποιοῦντες καλλίους γράφουσιν, but ὁμοίους here in effect means "like ourselves" (with καλλίους, cf. 53a16), as it does in 48a6, Διονύσιος δ' ὁμοίους εἴκαζεν, which Bywater himself notes to show "how inattentive Aristotle is at times to uniformity of language."

Aristotle's use of ὅμοιος in 53a5–10 is not in fact satisfactory. An Achilles or an Othello does not become more "like ourselves" because he has a fault, because he suffers δι' ἁμαρτίαν τινά: he is as great, σπουδαῖος, as much above ordinary humanity, in his fault as in his virtues.

most important element in it. As Vahlen put it (p. 29), such
re-creation of the material of legend or history is what makes
the poet.

Bywater, however, will have none of it; for him μίμησις "in
the case of a traditional story implies a certain free handling of
the materials to adapt them to the purpose of poetry," and he
cites that later passage, to which I referred in the preceding
chapter, in which Aristotle says that the poet is not entirely free
in handling his material when that comes from history or tradition. Klytaimnestra must be killed by Orestes, Eriphyle by
Alkmeon; but "he must invent and devise the right way of
treating the story," as though this, the right way of treating
the story, were only a little license granted to the poet though
denied the historian (Bywater translates 53b25, αὐτὸν δὲ εὑρίσκειν
δεῖ, "at the same time there is something left to the poet himself") and not the pith of the whole matter.[9] Gudeman's comment is no better. Indeed Aristotle might almost have said that
this is what marks the difference between poet and historian,
that it is the latter who is an "imitator" in Bywater's sense, in
that he must represent every incident that has happened within
his chosen field as it happened, and every person as true to life
as possible, whereas the poet's and the artist's function is something quite different. We must remember that practically all
Greek tragedies had, in fact, historical themes. Aristotle might
also have rejected portraiture and painting of actual landscape
as a portrayal of what is, not of what might be; as too particular, not generalized, and so less σπουδαῖον than true painting; we
ought hardly to be surprised if Aristotle had altogether rejected
imitative art, that is, art in which the likeness to the original is
strictly relevant.[10] We must not be misled by our inability to
translate μίμησις always by the same English word; why should
we expect a word in one language always to be represented by

[9] This was long ago emphasized by Wilamowitz in his edition of Euripides' *Herakles*,
p. 118; Gudeman, pp. 206–207, seems to misunderstand the matter.

[10] He could certainly condemn cheap imitative acting (61b29). There is much good
sense on this question to be found in Twining's essay, Vol. I, p. 42, note, and pp. 44–54.

precisely one word in another? In fact, in these and similar passages our nearest word is "representation."[11]

For Aristotle there is no doubt that the highest art, whether literary or visual, was that which was concerned with humanity, what men do and suffer, what happens to man, human fate, not with abstract patterns as in a carpet or a curtain, nor with landscape as such; the best art and the best poetry, epic or tragedy (or comedy), will thus "represent" life; but he does not, except in the broadest terms, say how it will "represent" it; that is to say, as far as his words go, the "representation" might be what we should call formal, or photographic, or impressionist, or cubist. It is quite wrong to suppose that he means "photographic."[12]

Nor did Plato believe that art is a form of imitation in that sense. Consider his purpose, his very austere purpose. His rulers are to look after, care for, the whole community, not to satisfy their own ambitions, their love of power and wealth; therefore they are to be denied the pleasures of property and family life. "You are not making them very happy," says Adeimantos. "We are not trying to make them happy," Socrates answers, "but to secure the greatest possible happiness for the whole community. It would be easy to make any class 'happy' in your sense of the word, by giving them a good time, rulers or farmers or cobblers, but would they be better rulers, farmers, and cobblers for that? That is, would they contribute their proper share to the community the better for living in luxury?"[13] The education of such rulers from their youth up must be seriously considered. "If our young men," says Socrates, "are to do their proper work in life" (which, remember, is to be *government*) "they must follow after these qualities wherever they may be found: excellence of form

---

[11] So Cornford, *Republic*, remarks prefatory to his Part V (*Repub.* x 595A–608B).

[12] Ross, p. 278. On p. 290 he says that the *Poetics* "marks the beginning of our deliverance from two mistakes—the tendency to confuse aesthetic with moral judgments, and the tendency to think of art as duplicative or photographic of reality." I agree, except for the words "marks the beginning." I do not think that Plato made either mistake.

[13] *Repub.* iv 419A ff.

in words, of musical expression and rhythm, and grace of form and movement. Such are to be found in every form of workmanship, such as painting, weaving, embroidery, architecture, the making of furniture, and also in the human frame and in all the works of nature. In all these, excellence of form may be present; they depend on the character of the soul in man."[14] "Le style c'est l'homme même," as Adam quotes in his note here. We may also observe in passing Plato's attitude to the manual arts, which we are told he utterly despised.[15] Plato goes on: "We must seek out those craftsmen whose instinct guides them to whatever is lovely and gracious, so that our young men, living in a wholesome climate, may drink in good from every quarter, whence, like a breeze bearing health from happy regions, some influence from noble works constantly falls upon eye and ear from childhood upward, and imperceptibly draws them into sympathy and harmony with the beauty of reason, whose impress they take. . . . Hence, Glaukon, the decisive importance of education in poetry and music; rhythm and harmony sink deep into the recesses of the soul and take the strongest root there, developing that grace of body and mind which is to be found only in one who is brought up in the right way." If he is brought up wrongly no grace will be there.

For one so sensitive as Plato was to all that can reach the eye and ear, and one so deeply concerned with the soul of man, it is not surprising that he was anxious about the kind of poetry and music, architecture and furnishing, that surrounded the young men who were later to be rulers and guardians of his city. It is a political anxiety, not one provoked by a theory of aesthetic.[16]

---

[14] *Repub.* iii 400D–401A. (The translation is based on Cornford's.)

[15] At vii 522B, αἲ τε γὰρ τέχναι βάναυσοί που ἄπασαι ἔδοξαν εἶναι, Cornford is surely misleading in translating "the manual crafts." They include *all* the different crafts, or skills, including the doctor's, the lawyer's, the merchant's, as well as those of the "artist" and the "craftsman," and the farmer—all those which are concerned particularly with the sensible objects of this world, of which the young of the guardian class may know something but which they are not to spend their lives practicing. Cf. 532C, 533B, 534D (and 532D for Plato's ironic exaggeration). Compare what Cornford himself says on the Marxist view of ancient philosophy in *The Unwritten Philosophy*, p. 130.

[16] So Cornford, p. 325, n. 2, though I doubt whether Plato was serious about the

He had two principal objections to Homer and tragedy. First, they aroused, stirred up, emotions that should be kept under control; they are dangerous, they may get out of hand. Secondly, they and the arts were concerned with human acts and passions, that is, with the objects of sense, and his rulers were to study in a world of pure intellect. They were to be denied inductive science too, not, I feel sure, because Plato did not know what inductive science was or was unconscious of the value of the observation of phenomena, but because this kind of study, that of the objects of sense perception, was not for his rulers. If they studied astronomy, it was to be astronomy without the stars. They must live wholly with dialectic, training themselves in logical thinking. Similarly they were denied poetry and art, though Plato shows on every page that he knows what poetry means. "It is not the thing said, but a way of saying things," as Housman put it. Just so; "rhythm and harmony sink deep into the recesses of the soul," and therein lies their danger. Good things, Plato knew, are likely to be dangerous—liberty, for example. For Plato too, poetry, music, and the visual arts are ways of expressing things. But he liked to provoke us by pretending at times that that is not what matters. For example: "the poet, knowing nothing more than how to represent appearances, can paint in words his picture of any craftsman so as to impress an audience which is equally ignorant (of that craft) and judges only by the form of expression; and the inherent charm of meter, rhythm, and musical setting is enough to make them think he has discoursed admirably about generalship or shoemaking or any other technical subject. Strip what the poet has to say of its poetical coloring and I think you must see what it comes to in plain prose." This is Plato pretending that poetry is trying to say that 2 plus 2 equals 4 (or something rather less useful than that) in a decorative way; that Shakespeare, when he wrote "I know a bank whereon the wild thyme

"extravagant claims made for the poets as moral teachers." Aristotle, of course, agreed with Plato that πολιτική must be supreme, but in the *Poetics* he is discussing not political but aesthetic theory.

blows," was only telling his neighbor where he could find thyme, which might be a more useful plant than the roses at which he was such a failure that he, Shakespeare, could hardly mention them in his poetry without pointing to the inevitable canker. We are reminded that Aristotle denied that Empedokles, writing on natural philosophy in verse, and good verse, was a poet. Plato was in no danger of thinking that Solon and Theognis were great poets because their moral sentiments were to be applauded. He treats painting in the same way. He knew well enough who were the great men in the arts and what their greatest works, as he knew and understood the greatest in literature; what does he therefore do? Does he take Polygnotos, who "painted men better than they really are," or Pheidias, who by his Zeus at Olympia had "added something to the received religion," and say why they, like Homer, must be crowned with garlands and, with the greatest respect, be shown the door? No, in his ironic way he prefers a man who paints a *bed*, and paints it with only one purpose, to deceive children and foolish adults into thinking that he has *made* a bed and so is a carpenter, a man who pretends to be a master of other crafts than his own. "So with Homer," he goes on. This is the parallel he draws with what was for him the noblest poetry, the music that could charm the soul. And we, in our solemn wisdom, repeat one after the other[17] that Plato's whole idea of art was the successfully deceptive representation of beds.[18]

---

[17] Except R. G. Collingwood, *Principles of Art*, pp. 46–52. It will be observed that I use the word "representation" in art very differently from him. He insisted, I do not know why, on taking it to mean the "photographic" copying of something in nature; he used "imitation" for the copying of another work of art.

[18] If we would consider more seriously the nature of "imitation" in art, we might put it thus, less ironically than Plato. The painter uses his eyes better than other men; he observes a line or a color which most others do not see at all and even those who use their eyes but have not the skill or practice in painting do not see so well. But it is not his purpose just to show these things to us who look at the picture so that we may exclaim: "I had not realized, that is, had not *seen*, that it was like this." That is Aristotle's οὗτος ἐκεῖνος (48b17)—a genuine pleasure, but not strictly relevant to the painter's art. Similarly with a close observation of human nature by a poet; some pictures and some writing will give pleasure by their nice observation of detail in man or in his surroundings. Aristotle saw the difference; Plato, I feel sure, did too, though at times he

Let us recall how he ends this discussion. "If we admit the honeyed muse of Homer into our city, then pleasure and pain will usurp the sovereignty of law and of the principles always recognized to be the best. . . . None the less, be it declared that if the poetry whose end is to give pleasure can show good reason why it should exist in a well-governed society, we for our part would welcome it back, because we are conscious of its charm, especially when it speaks through Homer's lips—only it would be a sin to betray what we believe to be the truth. If then poetry and her champions plead that she is no mere source of pleasure, but a benefit to society and human life, we shall listen favourably, for we shall clearly be the gainers if that can be proved. . . . But if it cannot, then we must take a lesson from the lover who

can pretend not. That, after all, is why he lays so much stress on the psychological effect of art, especially of tragedy and epic; his objections on that score have to be answered by the political theorist and the statesman, not by a theory of aesthetic, strictly so called.

I cannot agree with Collingwood that Plato makes a distinction throughout between "representative" poets (in Collingwood's sense) and others, and that in book iii of the *Republic* some "representative" poets, perhaps Aeschylus, are allowed to remain (all but those who represent trivial or disgusting things, "farmyard noises," 396B), but all are banished in book x, and only "non-representative" poets, as Pindar, would stay; nor that Aristotle with his *Poetics* was offering that defense of poetry which is meant to give pleasure, ἡ πρὸς ἡδονὴν ποιητικὴ καὶ ἡ μίμησις, which Sokrates asks for in 607CD, the social defense of poetry, the katharsis theory, being so small a part of his book. Collingwood translates ἡ πρὸς ἡδονὴν ποιητικὴ "amusement art" (which is always representational in his sense), which is correct only so far as Plato is banishing all ἡδονή for his guardians; but, of course, he is still paradoxical in implying that all pleasure is equally trivial. Aristotle meant by ἡδονή the pleasure properly given by poetry and art, just what Plato really meant, not "amusement." According to Collingwood (whose Plato must agree with *him*), Plato was contrasting the non-representational sculptures of Olympia with the representational Praxiteles of his own day (I doubt if the dates of Praxiteles will fit), and Aristotle, more philistine than Plato, was unconscious of any difference between them. But (1) certainly the Olympia sculptures are both "mimetic" in the Greek sense and πρὸς ἡδονὴν πεποιημένα; (2) had Plato meant any such distinction he would have said so, and why should he banish Aeschylus and keep the Master of Olympia? (3) Aristotle normally goes back to the fifth century or earlier for his great exemplars.

Professor Tate's articles in *CQ* XXII (1928), pp. 16–21, and XXVI (1932), pp. 161–169, are a much more serious discussion of μίμησις in Plato (if I, who am not a philosopher, may say so); but I am not sure that he would agree with what I have written here.

renounces at any cost a passion which he finds is doing him no good. The love of poetry of this kind, bred in us by our own most admired institutions, will make us kindly disposed to believe in her genuine worth, but so long as she cannot make good her defence we shall, as we listen, rehearse to ourselves the reasons we have just given as a countercharm to save us from relapsing into a passion which most people have never outgrown. . . . For, Glaukon, much is at stake, more than most people suppose; it is a choice between becoming a good man or a bad, and poetry, no more than wealth or power or honors, should tempt us to be careless of justice and virtue."[19] What high standards Plato had! He rejects not only "wealth and power and honors" for the rulers of the state he is setting up, but all that liberty and variety of life which he knew in Athens and describes with such sympathetic mockery (*Republic* viii 558AB, especially; see below, p. 176); and in recognizing the dangers of discussion of first principles among the young, even though such discussion is to be a major task of the rulers, he virtually rejects Sokrates himself and the life he had led in free Athens (vii 537A–539D). No wonder he rejects poetry too. But, because he understood its nature he would like it back; "we should obviously be the gainers if it returned."

Finally, when Aristotle makes his distinction between history and poetry, that the one deals with what has happened, the other with what would happen, and *therefore* poetry only can exhibit unity and logical coherence, while history cannot, are we to assume that for him (in Bywater's words) "a history is a chronicle, or register, of events taken just as they come in the order of time, however separate or disconnected they may have been in themselves"? It would seem so; he says that a story, in poetry, "should be based on a single action, one that is a complete whole in itself, with a beginning, middle, and end, so as to enable the work to produce its own proper pleasure with all the organic unity of a living creature, and not have its structure like a history. A history has to deal not with one action,

---

[19] *Repub.* x 607A–608B.

but with one period and all that happened in that to one or more persons, however disconnected the several events may have been";[20] and he instances the two battles of Salamis and Himera, which happened at the same time but did not arise from the same cause or converge to the same end. That looks clear enough, but is it the end of the matter for him? and would this seem to *us* an adequate description of Herodotos' *History?* Yet Aristotle had had him in mind earlier, and in this chapter too his example, the battles of Salamis and Himera, comes or might come from him. This is the problem we have to discuss in the next chapter, but meanwhile there are one or two problems of the *Poetics* worth discussing; though they are not strictly part of my theme, they do, I think, throw light on it.

APPENDIX TO CHAPTER III

I. "POETICS" 50b1

First a passage in the *Poetics* which is misunderstood in much the same way as those discussed above on Empedokles and on a historical subject used by a poet (47b18 and 51b28), namely, 50b1. Aristotle is emphasizing the supreme importance of plot, in comparison especially with character, as well as with thought and diction. You might, he says, have a number of speeches full of ἦθος and well written for style and thought, but if they are only strung together (ἐάν τις ἐφεξῆς θῇ) without logical connection like (apparently) events in a history, the tragedy will be a failure (50a29). Similarly in painting: εἰ γάρ τις ἐναλείψειε τοῖς καλλίστοις φαρμάκοις χύδην, οὐκ ἂν ὁμοίως εὐφράνειεν καὶ λευκογραφήσας εἰκόνα. Bywater translates: "where the most beautiful colours laid on without order will not give one the same pleasure as a simple black-and-white sketch of a portrait," and Gudeman agrees. But Vahlen was surely right that λευκογραφήσας is the contrast to χύδην, "after drawing an outline," as opposed to "at random" (which corresponds to ἐφεξῆς above), and εἰκόνα is sim-

---

[20] Bywater's translation, except for the difference in reading in 59a21-22, for which see above, p. 2, n. 2.

ply the finished picture (sc. εἰ ποιήσειε), as in 48b11, 15, not *portrait*. The argument is put exaggeratedly, indeed crudely, for colors are not beautiful in themselves as well-written speeches are, but only in relation to one another, and no one would take any pleasure in colors put on a canvas at random except those who like gorgeous technicolor, whereas you can get some pleasure from a series of well-made speeches, though not the pleasure proper to a tragedy. Only a picture which has been properly designed first, and only a tragedy with a good structure properly thought out, will give the proper pleasure.

Bywater explains: "A portrait, even though it be a mere monochrome in whites, will have a meaning, and give the mind the intellectual pleasure which accompanies the recognition of the meaning (cf. c. 4, 48b17); whereas a medley of beautiful colours has no meaning, and the pleasure it gives the beholder is of a wholly different order (cf. 48b18, οὐχ ᾗ μίμημα ποιήσει τὴν ἡδονὴν ἀλλὰ διὰ ... τὴν χροίαν)," and, Bywater implies, of an inferior kind. The passage to which Bywater here refers is the conclusion of that in c. 4 in which Aristotle gives as one explanation of the growth of representative art the pleasure of everybody, especially children, in recognizing the original of something "imitated," and in mimicry generally. "The reason of the delight in seeing the picture is that one is at the same time learning—gathering the meaning of things, e.g., that the man there [portrayed] is so-and-so—οὗτος ἐκεῖνος; for if one has not seen the thing before, one's pleasure will not be in the picture as an imitation of it, but will be due to the execution or colouring or some similar cause." But a medley of colors without meaning can give no pleasure; and what Aristotle has said in chap. 4 is that we, all of us, children and ordinary persons, take delight of some kind in learning and especially in learning from pictures by recognizing a likeness, "that is a horse," "that is Miss So-and-so," and he adds: "When we have not seen the object represented, we take pleasure in the colors or the technical skill or the like." A sensible, if not very profound, remark, intended to explain why we can take pleasure in, for example,

Titian's portrait of Pope Julius II, or "of an unknown man," or Canaletto's painting of eighteenth-century Venice or London; we do not look up other evidence to see if the likeness is exact. That, of course, is the true pleasure to be got from a painting; the other, the recognition of a likeness (what Bywater calls the intellectual pleasure), is accidental and spurious, natural to children and the simple-minded, and in all of us in some degree inevitable when faced with a painting of something or someone we are familiar with. Compare what was said above, p. 6, about the *Persai*. Aristotle understood this very well.[1]

II. GOODNESS OF CHARACTER

What does Aristotle mean by the statement that the tragic hero must be "good" (σπουδαῖος or χρηστός, cc. 2 and 15, *init*.)? Does he mean "of grand stature," as he appears to do when he is distinguishing between the personages of tragedy and those of comedy (c. 2), or does he mean "morally good"? The latter must, clearly, be the meaning in c. 15. "In the characters there are four points to aim at. First and foremost, that they shall be good (χρηστά). There will be character in a play if what a personage says or does reveals a certain moral purpose, and good character if the purpose so revealed is good."[2] Vahlen in his *Beiträge*, pp. 266–268, seems right in holding that σπουδαῖος, χρηστός, and ἐπιεικής are all synonyms for "morally good," but that σπουδαῖος has as well an aesthetic meaning, "of grand stature." W. D. Ross says that there is confusion between aesthetic and moral judgments (in his *Aristotle*, p. 290; cf. above,

---

[1] I may add that Castelvetro was surely right in putting the whole parenthesis (παραπλήσιον γάρ ἐστιν καὶ ἐπὶ τῆς γραφικῆς· εἰ γάρ τις ἐναλείψειε, κ.τ.λ.) after σύστασιν πραγμάτων, 50a32; not only does χύδην here answer to ἐφεξῆς in a29, but the "beautiful colors" correspond not to τὰ ἤθη, but to the "excellent thought and diction" of ῥήσεις ἠθικαί.

[2] I am not convinced that at 25, 61a4, it is correct to translate καλῶς ἢ μὴ καλῶς "morally right or not," instead of "well composed or not" ("poetically right," Butcher; cf. 47a10, 53a12, b26). Bywater compares *Eth. Nic.* iii 1.1111a4, but apparently similar passages in the *Ethics* and the *Poetics* are not necessarily to be interpreted as identical, any more than similar passages in the *Politics* and the *Poetics*. Cf. my paper on *Poet.* 15, 54a20, in a forthcoming number of *CQ*.

p. 57, n. 12). I am not sure; I think rather that Aristotle's statements about "goodness" in character, like those about history, are inadequate indeed, but not confused. He does mean that the tragic hero should be morally good, not faultless by any means, but good, noble. It is largely this which makes his fall through some fault in him (which itself is not just weakness or baseness, but springs from his goodness) tragic; and we can see what he means if we call to mind such tragic heroes as Oedipus, Elektra (Sophokles' Elektra), Antigone, Phaidra, above all Achilles in the *Iliad*, or, in Shakespeare, Othello, Lear, and Hamlet, especially Othello, a character which might almost have been expressly created in order to illustrate Aristotle's argument, while 1 and 2 *Henry VI* show very clearly the lack of tragic interest in characters which are just bad.

But Aristotle's statement is inadequate because it appears to exclude certain characters which are not morally good, but are tragic: Klytaimnestra, Medeia. Ross says indeed (p. 279) that Aristotle "has no conception of such a hero who, like Macbeth or Richard III or Milton's Satan, wins our interest by sheer intensity"; but this would argue (though the two Greek heroines make a rather different appeal) that *Agamemnon* and *Medea* were closed books to him, which I do not believe, any more than I believe that he had no understanding of Herodotos and Thucydides. The *Poetics* is by no means a complete statement of his theory. As Vahlen puts it, Aristotle might have said much more about different kinds of character, but "sollte man nicht glauben, Aristoteles habe der schöpferischen Kraft des Dichters ... nicht allzusinnlich unter die Arme greifen wollen?" It is, however, of great interest that in speaking of plots ὅταν ὁ σοφὸς μὲν μετὰ πονηρίας δ' ἐξαπατηθῇ, ὥσπερ Σίσυφος (one can imagine an *Iago*, with that bad man hero of the play) καὶ ὁ ἀνδρεῖος μὲν ἄδικος δ' ἡττηθῇ (as Richard III), 56a21, which are only "tragic in so far as they arouse human sympathy with even deserved misfortune" (Vahlen, pp. 277–278), the latter does not remind him of Klytaimnestra, especially in the Aeschylean presentation. She is wicked and she succumbs; she is also ἀνδρεῖος, contrary to the doctrine of c. 15, 54a23; and she is eminently tragic.

III. Aristotle and Comedy

It is commonly said that when Aristotle speaks of comedy as having given up ψόγος, personal invective, or ἡ ἰαμβικὴ ἰδέα, and taken to καθόλου ποιεῖν λόγους ἢ μύθους (49b8), "making stories of a universal, i.e., poetic kind," he is thinking of New Comedy by contrast with the Old Comedy of the fifth century, or, by those who think New Comedy began with Menander and is therefore later than Aristotle, of Middle Comedy in the second half of the fourth century; for, it is said, he thinks Old Comedy (with the exception of Krates: 49b7–9) to have been concerned with personal ψόγος, "abuse," not with the universal, and in that respect to be akin to history rather than to poetry. It will be remembered that he said that Homer, presumably in a lighter mood than usual—εὐτελέστερον,—opened a path to comedy with his *Margites* as he opened one to tragedy with the *Iliad*; and we can say that he did so because he produced not a personal invective, but a dramatization of the ridiculous (τὸ γελοῖον δραματο-ποιήσας). Yet we are told by Bywater and others that the great writers of comedy, the geniuses of the fifth century, and not they only but Archilochos also, did not follow him; it was left for the many small fry of the fourth century to write the first true comedies. This is so improbable that it is worth examining to see whether there is anything in Aristotle to justify it.[3]

The negative answer to the view that New Comedy is what Aristotle regards as comedy proper is that he does not mention a single writer or play from New or Middle Comedy. Since he says little of comedy altogether in what remains of the *Poetics*, this negative is not decisive, though it suggests that some justification of the current view is needed; but when we observe that when he is talking about comedy, as at the end of c. 2 and at the beginning of c. 5, he refers only to comedy representing people in a manner worse than the reality, and when he wants instances of poetry representing people like ourselves, he does not men-

---

[3] Twining, it may be recalled, took a much more sensible view.

tion New Comedy, our doubts are justified. For this was just one of the most novel and striking features of New Comedy; "Oh, Menander and Life, which of you copied the other?" Positively, when Aristotle wants the typical writer of comedies to bracket with the typical writer of tragedies, Aristophanes is the one who comes to mind, with Sophokles; or Epicharmos (48a27, 33); always the fifth century.[4]

In c. 4 (48b23–32) Aristotle tells us something of the origin of poetry, of what we should call "conscious" or "self-conscious" poetry, from improvisations (αὐτοσχεδιάσματα), an anticipation of much recent theory, the improvisations being either hymns and enkomia or ψόγοι, personal invectives; the former are the ancestors of the epic, the latter of *Margites* and of Archilochos and his ἴαμβοι. The ψόγοι (like the ἐγκώμια) were personal, not in any way "a portrayal of human life" and so not poetry, though they were in verse, but didactic like Empedokles' verses. Comedy developed partly from these ψόγοι, partly from the phallic songs, as tragedy from the enkomia and from the dithyramb and the satyr plays; it was as clearly καθόλου πεποιημένη, "generalized," as tragedy. We might make a genealogical tree rather like those we draw of manuscript descent, exhibiting cross influences, thus:

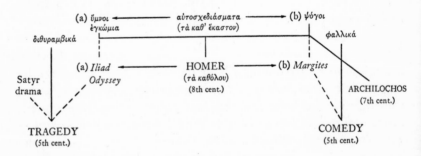

Old Comedy was as "creative," i.e., as generalized, as New.

---

[4] Bywater's note on Epicharmos, 48a33, is really inconsistent with his own views of what Aristotle meant by comedy.

Bywater, Hamilton Fyfe, Gudeman, and others suppose that Aristotle is making the distinction between Old and New (or Middle) Comedy, between the personal abuse, ψόγοι, of real individuals, Kleon, Sokrates, Hyperbolos in the former, and the generalized abuse or mockery of "the greedy man" (*L'Avare*), the rascally servant, or the vain young man, in the latter. But, in the first place, the introduction of real characters is exceptional, certainly in Aristophanes; we have Kleon in *The Knights*, Sokrates in *The Clouds*, and perhaps Euripides in *Thesmophoriazousai*, and, in quite a different manner, in *The Frogs*; Lamachos and Euripides in *The Acharnians* and Agathon in *Thesmophoriazousai* are minor characters. In the rest, the characters, where they are finely drawn, are as generalized as in tragedy: Dikaiopolis and Trygaios, Peithetairos, Lysistrate, above all Philokleon (his very name is a generalization, *the* follower of Kleon, not simply "one of Kleon's party," but a devoted follower), as well as lesser characters like Strepsiades and Pheidippides. Secondly, when he does introduce real characters, except when he does it to make the already extravagant seem yet more extravagant, he generalizes *them*, i.e., strips them of their nonessential, purely incidental characteristics, "the various accidents which coexist in the concrete individual," to quote Bywater; Kleon in *The Knights* is a *portrait*, but he is also *the* demagogue, Lamachos is indeed the prototype of all future *milites gloriosi*. Aeschylus' *Persai*, as I can only repeat, is not the less generalized than *Agamemnon* or *The Seven* because Xerxes, a living contemporary, is a character in it and the messenger's speech is the account of a real battle. (Agamemnon and Eteokles are also historical characters, but in a different sense, as we saw in our first chapter.) Where we do find relics of the old ψόγοι in Aristophanes is in the short songs of personal abuse of individuals which are, almost always, irrelevant to the play in which they occur, and are generally not abuse of public men for public deeds, but of private individuals for personal immoralities, as of Ariphrades in *The Knights*, 1280–1289. Apart from these little outbursts, Old Comedy, like Archilochos and

Homer's *Margites*, οὐ ψόγον ἀλλὰ τὸ γελοῖον ἐδραματοποίει (48b37), "produced not an invective but a dramatic picture of the ridiculous."

Krates, it is said, was distinguished from his fellow poets of the Old Comedy. He was, in two ways: (1) Aristotle so distinguished him on the ground that he was the first to drop the ἰαμβικὴ ἰδέα, the iambic form, and to make stories, i.e., plots, of a general type, the first comic dramatist who can properly be said to have *constructed* a play instead of writing a series of comic scenes, which, of course, does not mean that others, Kratinos, Aristophanes, Eupolis, and the rest, did not follow him. (2) As Aristophanes so clearly implies in that fine chorus in *The Knights* (518 ff., 537–540), Krates did not primarily take public affairs as his province, as Kratinos and many others often did, and as Aristophanes specifically claims that he did in the *parabasis* of *The Wasps* (1015 ff.) which is so oddly repeated in *The Peace* (739 ff.). Aristophanes took important public men and public affairs as his special theme; Krates may well have been gentler as well as quieter than the others and so in quite another sense too may have dropped the "iambic idea" which is, in that sense, the inspiration of Aristophanes; he may thus have been the forerunner of New Comedy. But that does not mean that *The Knights* is any less a λόγος καθόλου πεποιημένος (a story made generic or universal), or that Aristotle thought Archilochos a writer of primitive ψόγοι and Aristophanes no true representative of comedy, τῶν τό γελοῖον δραματοποιησάντων. *The Knights* is made διὰ τῶν εἰκότων ("a series of probable incidents"; 51b13); it is not a story of τί Κλέων ἔπραξεν ἢ ἔπαθεν, *what in reality Kleon did or suffered* (51b11), and I am sure Aristotle did not think that it was. We must be careful how we translate these many words which like μίμησις itself have more than one meaning, including meanings of wider and of narrower scope; in c. 4, for instance, after saying that Homer was the ancestor, or the inspirer, of both tragedy and comedy, Aristotle goes on: "As soon as Tragedy and Comedy appeared, those naturally drawn to the one line of poetry became writers of comedies instead of iambs, and those naturally drawn to the other, writers of tragedies instead of epics, because these new modes of art were grander and of more esteem than the old." Here κωμῳδοποιοὶ ἐγένοντο certainly means Old Comedy, and ἴαμβοι, corresponding to ἔπη, here means Archilochos, not primitive ψόγοι.

I would add a word about the *names* of characters in tragedy and comedy, for Aristotle expresses himself awkwardly when he says of the distinction between poetry and history that the former deals with universals, that is, with what *such or such a kind* of man will do in such or such circumstances, "which is the aim of poetry, *just adding proper names to the characters.*" This at first sight may seem to mean that it deals with individuals as history does, especially as most of the names in tragedy were historical. It is, of course, true that in an epic or tragedy the universal is *embodied* in individuals, but what Aristotle must mean here and later in c. 17 (55b3), if he is talking sense, is that the dramatist must make up his mind what sort of a play he wants first, e.g., a story like that of *Iphigeneia in Tauris*; he cannot mean that he thinks out the whole story for himself as an original plot in general terms (κόρη τις, ὁ ἀδελφός, βαρβάρων βασιλεύς), and then exclaims, all surprised, "Why, Iphigenia, Orestes, and Thoas will be suitable names." We do not suppose that Shakespeare, as he went home in the evening from Blackfriars, said to himself: "I want to do a play about a weak and foolish king, quite unequal to his position but a likable man, attacked and, inevitably, broken by efficient ruthless rebels"; and when he got home, plotted his play, and not till then opened his Holinshed and cried out: "Why, Richard II is just the king I wanted." On the contrary, he was writing history plays; he was reading the chronicles, and when he came to Richard, "There," he must have felt, "is something that I can do, namely, make a tragedy out of these chronicle dramas by putting my Richard into it," by what Bywater calls "a certain free handling of the story." So obviously Homer, but so also Sophokles. He knew the Theban story from his childhood, and his mind would work something like this: "I am going to make Kreon the sort of king (βασιλεύς τις) who would issue an edict which, as the world goes, would seem not to be a bad one, by which to distinguish the patriot Eteokles from his traitorous and vicious brother, and who, secondly, would insist in the interests of law and order that edicts be obeyed; and I am going to make Antigone the sort of girl (κόρη τις) who would pay the last rites to a dead brother no matter how badly he had behaved in life. Thence there will be tragedy, that is how things would happen, οἷα ἂν γένοιτο." Next he would say: "But how can I manage the *plot*? That is the important thing."[5]

Comedy does in a sense add names, though some that imply types, Philokleon, Lysistrate, Peithetairos, Euelpides, are so much part of the plot that they must have been there from the beginning. Even Lamachos is nearly one of these. But Menander takes names from life, occasionally to describe characters, especially of the military type, Thrasonides, Polemon, but generally ordinary names which he or another had made conventional by the assumption that a Moschion and Pamphile are young, a Smikrines old, and so on—a possible convention because in a *play* which, unlike a history, has nothing earlier than its beginning and nothing subsequent to its end, Smikrines has never been young, and Moschion and Pamphile never grow old.[6]

---

[5] By "the universal" here, and κόρη τις etc., Aristotle does not, of course, mean simply general types of character (Sophokles' characters are not "general types"); he means that a universal truth is embodied in a story about particular individuals. See Butcher, pp. 192–194; Ross, p. 278.

[6] In 51b12 ἐπὶ μὲν οὖν τῆς κωμῳδίας ἤδη τοῦτο δῆλον γέγονεν, ἤδη means, I feel sure, "at this stage of the argument," "at once," not as Bywater, "now that the New Comedy has taken the place of the Old," nor "as soon as comedy (i.e., Old Comedy) began with Krates"; and οἱ ἰαμβοποιοί means Archilochos, not Old Comedy; nor as Gudeman, if I understand him rightly, "It is by now agreed by all for comedy, but not for tragedy."

IV

Herodotos

WOULD IT BE an adequate, or in any significant
way an accurate, description of Herodotos' *History* to call it "a
chronicle of events taken just as they came in order of time,
however separate and disconnected they may have been in
themselves" (which is Bywater's account of Aristotle's view,
Poetics 51a36)? The question is a rhetorical one, of the kind
that demands and receives the answer, No. (Aristotle might perhaps have retorted, "I did not mean this to be my last word about
history.") "As an instance of such a disconnected event," says
Bywater in another note (to 59a23), "Aristotle cites Gelo's defeat of the Carthaginians in 480; it happened about the same
time—Herodotus 7, 166 says on the same day—as the Battle
of Salamis, but it obviously had no connexion with that battle,
or with the issue of the Persian War. And the same would have
to be said, if it had taken place just before or just after Salamis
(ἐν τοῖς ἐφεξῆς χρόνοις, a27). In this way Aristotle reasserts the
point on which he has insisted in the earlier chapters (8, 51a27;
10, 52a20), that two events may come in succession without
forming part of one single action." Is this an adequate description of Herodotos' account of Salamis and Himera? The answer
is again, clearly, No; but it is worth looking into the matter
more closely. We must remember that Herodotos has been cited
by Aristotle as the typical historian, and Salamis and Himera
are important episodes in his story.

Herodotos does not, in fact, narrate the battle of Himera immediately before or immediately after Salamis, nor at the same
time, but in quite a different context. It was an unfortunate
example for Aristotle to choose. For the historian, in book vii,

relating in detail the slow, impressive march of Xerxes' millions
from the interior of Asia, by Sardis and the Hellespont, Doriskos
and the canal through the isthmus of Athos, heralded by an
eclipse of the sun, when in a clear sky day became night (vii
37.2; but in fact the eclipse took place the year before), brings
them at last to the confines of Greece. By a stroke of art he then
makes Xerxes discuss matters with the exiled Demaratos of
Sparta, who tells him something of the quality of men he is
likely to meet in battle (vii 101), and that gives us the transition to the Greek side. How are things faring there? After
naming those Greek states that were for surrender and some
other details, Herodotos tells us about the resisting states, how
they had taken counsel together (vii 145). They had decided on
three things: first, to end all wars among themselves; second, to
send men to spy out the strength of the enemy forces while
they were still on the march from Sardis to the Hellespont;[1]
third, to send to Gelon, the powerful prince who controlled
nearly all Sicily, to urge a united front against the Persians.
This, in due course, gives him occasion for a digression on the
origin of the power of the Deinomenidai and its culmination in
Gelon's monarchy at Syracuse; then for the account of the
meeting between him and the delegates from eastern Greece
(vii 157). Gelon, scornful of their sudden desire for friendship,
is yet ready to send help (generous help: food for all and many
troops) on conditions: he must be supreme commander of the
Greek forces. The Spartan delegate could not tolerate this:
"Agamemnon, son of Pelops"—the old commander-in-chief
against Troy,—"would turn in his grave. But you Syracusans
may have the honor of serving under Spartan command." Gelon
answered: "Very well, I will not sink so low as to answer rudeness by rudeness, but give me the command of all the naval
forces." But here the Athenian delegate intervened: "We came

---

[1] These spies were caught and were about to be put to death when Xerxes intervened and said: "On the contrary, show them everything, everything they can want
to see, and then send them back home, so that their countrymen will learn how powerful my forces are, and will at once surrender; *we* shall not gain anything by killing three
men." It is not often that espionage is treated so sensibly.

here to ask for the assistance of an armed force, not for a commander. *We* have much the largest navy of all the Greek states; we are content to be commanded by a Spartan; but if the Spartan is prepared to surrender his command, it must be to us and to no one else." "Then begone without any help from me," said Gelon; "it looks as though you have plenty of commanders but no troops to command."

Herodotos, however, goes on to relate that Gelon would probably have sent help against Xerxes if it had not been for the threat of an invasion from Carthage owing to internecine strife at Himera. The tyrant there had been driven out and had called in the aid of the Carthaginians; they responded and sent a great force under Hamilcar. A stubborn battle was fought between them and the greater part of the Greek forces of Sicily under Gelon and Theron; this ended in a complete victory for the Greeks on the same day, it was said in Sicily, as that on which the Greeks, fighting against Xerxes, won the battle of Salamis. (There is the implication that this particularity is to add point to the Sicilian reason for having sent no help to the eastern Greeks.) That is Herodotos' brief account of the battle of Himera, told before ever Xerxes had set foot in Greece, before the story of Thermopylai and Artemision, and long before that of Salamis, and no further reference is made to it. Not a case of "a chronicle of events taken just as they came in the order of time, however disconnected and separate they may be in themselves"; these two events are not related by Herodotos in order of time, and they are connected by him the one with the other.

For myself I do not think this particular *epeisodion* as well managed as most of those in Herodotos' *History* are, and besides it would certainly be pedantic to quarrel with Aristotle for giving so unfortunate an example. He had read very many historians, as he had read hundreds of tragedies and comedies, and not only the few that remain to us (as Gudeman reminds us, wisely), and he may be forgiven for forgetting Herodotos for the moment; or, perhaps, he was thinking of some other historian, even though Herodotos had been his typical example a few chapters back. But it *is* reasonable to complain that Aristotle did not observe in this context, where he is comparing poetry and history, that this sort of arrangement of his material is habitual with Herodotos, that he regularly forsakes the chronological for a logical order, as regularly as Plutarch does for his purposes, and not only that, but that here in this brief account of the battle of Himera he can anticipate his later story of the outcome of the battle of Salamis, the Greek victory, as readily as Homer in the *Iliad* can refer to Achilles' early death and to the destruction of Troy and in the *Odyssey* to Odysseus' further wanderings from Ithake after his success against the suitors and his restoration to his home and family. Of course, he observes in general, particularly in the last three books which constitute the climax of his narrative, Xerxes' invasion and defeat, the chronological sequence, just as Plutarch the biographer does; but so too does the poet, the creative artist, the writer of fiction in the *Odyssey* as elsewhere, despite the long "flashback" that we have in Odysseus' narrative of the earlier adventures at the banquet with Alkinoös. Thucydides, with his insistence on chronological order, has a different method of keeping to logic; I shall be discussing him later, but here I may remind you that he too can anticipate; the much later effects of Perikles' death, of Brasidas' victories, of Alkibiades' lawlessness, are all told well in advance of the events. Of Herodotos we can say that it is one of the most clearly marked features of his *History*, of its whole structure and "economy," that it is not a chronicle in Bywater's sense of the word, nor apparently in Aristotle's; that it is a triumph not of chronological but of *logical*, that is, for Aristotle in this context, *poetical* arrangement; that, as we should more probably say, it is a work of art, its author an accomplished artist, the "poet" of his plot. After all, ποιητής, in some of its uses, *means* "artist."

We can dismiss from our minds the idea that Aristotle in this passage, or these two passages (cc. 9 and 23), was thinking particularly of "bare chronicles," like the local histories of Greece, *Atthides*, *Milesiaka*, and the rest (if these were "bare chronicles," which is doubtful, as Dr. Jacoby has recently made clear in his *Atthis*), some of which were written in Athens when Aristotle was there. The argument is often urged as if his range was limited to his contemporaries, in comedy and even in tragedy no less than in history; but in fact, as I have said before, when he wants a typical representative of a form of literature or art he always goes back to the fifth century (or earlier, as to Archilochos or Homer), and for history his representative is Herodotos. Even if he had contemporary historians in mind, these will have been such men as Ephoros and Theopompos, who, whatever their defects and however "unphilosophic" their writings, were certainly not "bare chroniclers" in the sense of men who related events just as they came in order of time, and did nothing else.[2] I made the statement in the first chapter that when Aristotle says that historians must deal with a period of time and cover all the events within that period, he might have been thinking of Kratippos, Xenophon, and Theopompos, all of whom began where Thucydides left off (pp. 3 f. above), and that when he gives us his example of the particularity of history (which relates not οἷον ἂν γένοιτο, "what would happen," but τί ἐγένετο, "what happened"), namely, τί ᾿Αλκιβιάδης ἔπραξεν ἢ τί ἔπαθεν, "what Alkibiades did or what happened to him" (a fifth-century example again!), he could have had any one of these three,[3] or Thucydides himself, in mind. But of them only Xenophon or Kratippos, the unknown, might in order to sustain the argument be described as a chronicler.

I have already mentioned as an example, an obvious one, of the difference in aim and purpose of poetry and history, the battles of Thermopylai and Plataia in *The Persians* and in Herodotos; we should have criticized the latter if he had treated

---

[2] It will be remembered that Ephoros is specifically said to have written κατὰ γένος (e.g., Sikeliot and Italiote history separately from that of Greece proper), not just in the chronological order of events, and that in a universal history. This in itself would hardly save him from being a chronicler and nothing more, but it should save him from the imputation of having written of Salamis and Himera on the same page because the battles occurred at the same time.

[3] Especially Kratippos: cf. Plutarch, *de Glor. Ath.* I, p. 345D.

them in so summary a fashion as Aeschylus does. But we can, of course, go further than this; had Herodotos behaved so, we should not even be in a position to criticize him, for it is he who supplies us with the facts which would enable us to make this hypothetical criticism of him and to refuse to criticize, because we understand, Aeschylus. It was his purpose, his scientific purpose, to prevent the facts of the wars between Greece and Asia and their causes from disappearing from the memories of man: ὡς μήτε τὰ γενόμενα ἐξ ἀνθρώπων τῷ χρόνῳ ἐξίτηλα γένηται, μήτε ἔργα μεγάλα τε καὶ θωμαστά, τὰ μὲν Ἕλλησι τὰ δὲ βαρβάροισι ἀποδεχθέντα, ἀκλεᾶ γένηται, τά τε ἄλλα καὶ δι' ἣν αἰτίην ἐπολέμησαν ἀλλήλοισι.[4] He must, like all scientists, widen the boundaries of knowledge, or at least prevent them from contracting, and must look for the causes of events. Such too had been the aims of all *chroniclers*, including those in verse who preceded Homer: they recorded κλέα ἀνδρῶν, records of men (compare Herodotos' ὡς μήτε . . . ἀκλεᾶ γένηται, "so that the great deeds do not go unrecorded"),[5] τὰ γενόμενα (as Herodotos), not οἷα ἂν γένοιτο. It is the poet, Homer, Aeschylus or Sophokles, or Aristophanes, who, for his purpose, relates οἷα ἂν γένοιτο. But what is important to us now is the manner in which Herodotos carries out his purpose.

It will make my meaning clearer, perhaps, if I say first that Macan's view seems to me a probable one, namely, that Herodotos wrote, or at least planned to write, books vii–ix, substantially in the form in which we have them, i.e., the history of Xerxes' invasion, of the years 480–479, before he thought of the elaborate account of the Persian Empire as it appears in the first five books. It is not demonstrable, it is not capable of proof, and I differ altogether from J. E. Powell's view that such problems are *like* those of mathematics, capable of exact proof.[6]

---

[4] I am not one of those who subscribe to the recent view that ἔργα here means buildings or works of art as opposed to actions, which are included in τὰ γενόμενα. I believe ἔργα to be used here as by Thucydides i 21 and 22.1. See Schwartz, *Das Geschichtswerk des Thukydides* (1919), p. 20, note.

[5] So Schwartz, *loc. cit.*

[6] *The History of Herodotus* (Cambridge, 1929), preface.

Macan's position is, however, I think, probable and more illuminating than others; it throws more light on the *History* as a whole.

What then, says Herodotos, was the *meaning* of this assault on Greece, and what was this Asiatic power which made it? He is going to describe later all the constituent elements of Xerxes' huge and many-colored, many-weaponed army: how came he to command so large and heterogeneous a force? Persians themselves and Medes, Egyptians, Phoenicians, Assyrians, Cappadocians; Indians, Armenians, Sakai; Phrygians, Lydians, many Greek states (those in Asia Minor and the islands); and Thracians and Macedonians from Europe. It is not sufficient to say that "the war was between the Greeks and the βάρβαροι"; who were these βάρβαροι, these foreigners? Or, as in commemorative epitaphs, "when we fought the Mede," what does the word Μῆδοί properly convey? This is what Herodotos will explain: what do we mean by βάρβαροι (in this context), and how did the empire, and its control by the Persians, come about?

We begin with the humorous little preface about the mutual ravishments of women. The Persians admit that Asia began it in the persons of the Phoenicians who carried off Io; the Greeks retaliated first by the seizure of Europe from Sidon, then of Medea from Kolchis: one up to the Greeks. Then Asia made it all square when Paris eloped with Helen, but the Greeks, say the Persians, were the first who were so mad as to start a major war (the Trojan) for so inadequate a cause. After this short preface, which with his usual skepticism about the earliest periods of Greek history he dismisses as all uncertain and unimportant, Herodotos recounts the first historical conflict that he knows of between Greece and Asia, and that was between the Greeks of Ionia, on the Asiatic mainland, and their neighbors, the non-Greeks of Lydia. What sort of country is Lydia, he asks, and what sort of people are the Lydians? There is a divergence here from his usual practice, which is not to describe a country and its inhabitants till they come into conflict with Persia and pass under her control, since that is his main theme:

what was this huge empire? Here, understandably enough, he begins with Greece's closest neighbors and first enemies.[7] In the course of a brief description and history of Lydia he comes to Croesus, and at once is able to tell the story in a way to illustrate his "philosophy of history," as we rather pompously call it; we thus learn something of it at the beginning of his work. Great prosperity, great happiness, is dangerous, slippery (σφαλερόν τι). It is in this respect like power (iii 53.4), but it does not have to be accompanied by wickedness in any form, pride, arrogance, selfish ambition, in order to be dangerous.

Solon in the famous "interview" makes this clear. Croesus in Herodotos is an altogether sympathetic character, courteous, kind, taking a simple pleasure in his vast wealth, generous to a degree, not generous simply with his riches, but generous-minded, as he so conspicuously shows in his treatment of the unfortunate Adrestos. He is free from all arrogance and pride, "a good man, beloved of the gods" (i 87.2), but he was vain and did not think that such *success* could have a fall; but it could. A great monster of a boar ravaged a distant part of his kingdom; that would not seriously or for long interrupt his prosperity, and it did not. A hunt ended the boar's life—but at the cost of the life of his only son,[8] killed accidentally by the man whom he had so generously befriended (the most moving and most Homeric story in Herodotos). He was not tyrannical either, not blown with pride at the present greatness and prosperity of his kingdom; but its power too he thought invulnerable—or, more accurately, he did not remember its vulnerability. So, light-

---

[7] I am oversimplifying; the problems of Herodotos' *Lydiaka* are many. They are well discussed by De Sanctis, *Studi di Storia* (Florence, 1951), pp. 47–71 (*Rivista di Filol.* LXIV [1936], pp. 1–14).

[8] There is a curious little detail here. Croesus had, in fact, another son, who was deaf and dumb and was to make a dramatic entrance into the story later (i 85). There we are told he was ἐπιεικής, ἄφωνος δέ, and that Croesus τὸ πᾶν ἐς αὐτὸν ἐπεποιήκεε. In the story of Adrestos he is dismissed summarily 34.3 and 38.2 (εἷς γάρ μοι μοῦνος τυγχάνεις ἐὼν παῖς· τὸν γὰρ δὴ ἕτερον, διεφθαρμένον τὴν ἀκοήν, οὐκ εἶναί μοι λογίζομαι). A piece of history, from a "chronicle," has been ignored in one or other of the two stories, like Neoptolemos, son of Achilles, in the *Iliad* (above, p. 37).

heartedly, without due thought, yet not without making the ordinary military preparations—for he was no fool like Kambyses, and his campaign was not like that foolish and savage one against the long-lived Ethiopians in iii 25—without, we repeat, due consideration of the nature of his task, he challenged the might of Persia, and he and his country were utterly overthrown. He had a complaint, a justifiable complaint, one would say, against Delphi for encouraging him, but that does not excuse his own frivolity of mind. Not till then, after the private and the public loss, did he remember Solon. Cyrus too, without thought, was ready to follow traditional custom and burn his captive, Croesus, on a great pyre, to celebrate his triumph, till he was told the story of Solon's visit; then, reflecting that he also was but a man, that he was putting to the flames another man who had been as prosperous as himself till now, and remembering how uncertain are human affairs, he repented and was anxious to have Croesus rescued from the pyre; but too late. Too late, that is, for mortal aid, but Apollo saved Croesus "when from a clear sky and in a still air, clouds gathered suddenly, and such a tempest broke forth, such rain fell, that the fire was quenched." Men do not *think*, says Herodotos.

I will interpolate here a word about the beliefs of Herodotos, such as this, that prosperity is a slippery thing, and the more important extension of it, that power is even more dangerous because it is corrupting, because it leads to *hubris*. It is wrong to call this primitive in the sense that it is a belief characteristic of primitive, undeveloped peoples which had survived all the changes in Greece from the eighth or seventh centuries and was just accepted by the conservative Herodotos, or, if you prefer it, which proves that the Greeks of the fifth century were in general still primitive. It is equally misleading to say that to have such a belief argues a mind that does not think for itself. On the contrary, I am sure that it is the result of *observation* of human affairs by Herodotos. Not by him alone; he was a child of the age, and Aeschylus, for one, had thought along similar lines, and Thucydides was to say much the same thing after him, though in a profounder way. But Herodotos had known the thing happen over and over again, men prosperous but yet unhappy, powerful yet brought to the ground. In the sixth century there had been Croesus and so many of the Greek tyrants whose rule had been overthrown, and in Aeschylus' manhood and when Herodotos was a boy there had been the tremendous and wholly improbable experience of the overthrow of the mighty Xerxes. This, I say, was a matter of observation. The Greeks often *interpreted* the phenomenon by the theory of divine φθόνος, "jealousy" or "envy," though I would not express this so simply (at least not for Aeschylus or Herodotos) as Dodds, for example, has done. "The gods," he writes, "resent any success, any happiness, which might for a moment lift our mortality above its mortal status, and so encroach on their prerogative." I should prefer the emphasis to be rather, "The gods and men are equally part of the order of nature and each have their sphere" (Pindar's "one race there is of the gods and one of men, and we are all children of Earth") "and men should not attempt to step out of theirs." Nor do I think "the crushing sense of human ignorance and human insecurity, the dread of divine *phthonos*, the dread of *miasma*,"[9] appropriate to the self-confidence of Aeschylus and his generation or to the free spirit of Herodotos (whose Croesus has no *fear* of the taint brought by Adrestos). *We* may interpret the phenomenon differently and may get nearer to the truth, but that does not make Aeschylus or Herodotos primitive. Indeed, the defeat of Xerxes is one of those happenings which Aristotle classed as possible but improbable, and for that reason might have been regarded as an unsuitable subject for epic or tragedy, and it is only the genius of Aeschylus and Herodotos which has made it seem also probable, because, each in his own way, they have lifted it from the sphere of the local and the temporal, just the story of a Greek victory over barbarians, into that of the permanent, the record of the fate of a man and a people who have been guilty

---

[9] *The Greeks and the Irrational*, Sather Lectures XXV (1950), pp. 29, 75.

of just that kind of pride which is both wrong in itself and also leads to a fall.[10]

There are two other beliefs held by Herodotos and his contemporaries which are not generally recognized as so primitive because they are humane, though hardly the result of observation: the belief, namely, that Zeus punishes the perjurer, and the belief that he helps the suppliant. He punishes, that is, the *successful* perjurer, because *ex hypothesi* the human judges have failed, have been deceived by the perjury, as in the Herodotean story (vi 86) of Glaukos, son of Epikydes; and he protects the helpless suppliant, the outcast and the beggar, because *ex hypothesi* he cannot help himself, as in the Herodotean story of Paktyes the Lydian in Kyme (i 157–160). It is easy to deceive humans by a false oath, and the easiest thing in the world to injure the helpless, to steal from a blind beggar; but our moral sense repudiates it, and so (it is wishful thinking, perhaps) we say that the gods will in their own way punish the wrongdoer.

To get back from this philosophy to the structure of the book: we have had mention of Cyrus and his Persians; who were they? Herodotos tells us expressly that that is the question he must now answer (i 95). It is the more pertinent because Cyrus, in absorbing Lydia into his empire, took in those Greek cities of Asia which had been subject to Croesus, paying him tribute.

We are told, therefore, first of the Medes and the rise of the royal house among them and their conquest of Assyria and half of Anatolia; then of Cyrus himself, half-Median of the royal house, with the Persians now taking the lead over the Medes,

---

[10] Contrast with this the story which Aristotle gives as an example of the marvelous (*Poetics* 52a3): "The incidents of a tragedy will have a greater effect if they occur unexpectedly, yet plainly as a consequence of one another; there is more to impress the mind with wonder (τὸ θαυμαστόν) than if they happened by mere chance. Even matters of chance are more impressive if there is an appearance of design, as it were, in them, as for instance the statue of Mitys at Argos killed the author of Mitys' death by falling on him when he was a spectator at a festival. An incident like this we think to be not without a meaning, not to happen simply haphazard (οὐκ εἰκῇ γίγνεσθαι)." It is, we think, so apt, so suitable therefore for a story. If Herodotos had known it, he would have told it, just for that reason, though he might have added: "I do not believe it to be true."

and the conquest of Babylon. All Mesopotamia, then all Anatolia, and Syria, are included within the empire; we have descriptions of the countries themselves as they come within the
compass of the history.[11] Cyrus was succeeded by his son,
Kambyses, who invaded Egypt. What was Egypt? Thus we
have the long, the overlong account in book ii. Afterward follows the story of the conquest of Egypt and of the brief but
animated reign of the mad king. Then the accession of Darius,
the great and wise; more conquests as far east as India, more
descriptions of countries and peoples; then the invasion of the
Balkan peninsula (more Greek cities brought into subjection),
the failure in Scythia (what is Scythia? why did the expedition
fail?); the conquest of Cyrenaica, which was Greek (how did it
come to be Greek?); the submission of Macedonia; till at last
we come to the revolt of the Ionian Greeks against the great
empire, after which the history of Greece and Asia is inter-
woven, forming one story: the story of the war. There is still
much to tell before the description of Xerxes' armed forces in
book vii, and this includes the campaign of Marathon and the
death of Darius; but the description of the armed forces assumes all the first six books and, in a sense, is their justification;
this was the power and this its ruler that invaded Greece and
was defeated.

The description takes the form of a muster of all the troops
at Doriskos in Thrace, army and navy, regiment by regiment,
contingent by contingent, nation by nation, with their numbers
(grossly exaggerated) and their commanding officers, just after
the manner of the catalogue of the ships in the *Iliad*, all in-

---

[11] As is well known, the account of Assyria is promised (i 106, 184), but none exists in
our text. Powell thinks that Herodotos had written it but cut it out (and other parts
besides) "in order to bring the Persian and Greek parts of the work into balance," when
he was expanding his *Persian History* into the *History* that we know—τὰ Περσικά coming first in order, according to Powell (*The History of Herodotus*, pp. 18–23; *Translation*
[Oxford, 1949], p. xiv). Perhaps; but if Herodotos had desired better balance, it is in the
long book ii, the account of Egypt, that cuts would have been made. As stated above, I
prefer Macan's view that Herodotos planned the narrative of the Persian War first;
but see also De Sanctis, *Studi di Storia*, pp. 21–45 (*Rivista di Filol.* LIV [1926], pp.
289–309).

spected and counted by Xerxes. Then they move slowly on, a great army that eats up the country for its food and dries up rivers for its drink. But shortly before this Herodotos has given us an account of the march of the whole land force from Sardis, where it had finally mustered, to the bridges over the Hellespont, for the bridges mark the point where the invasion proper begins, after which there can be no turning back except in triumph with the spoils and the prisoners, or in defeat,—which is unthinkable. This is how he does it (vii 40):

In the van marched the baggage train and the animals; then the fighting force, of all the nations together; after half of them had passed there was a gap, for none of these came in contact with the King. He was preceded by a thousand horse, chosen from all the Persian ranks, then by a thousand spearmen, also chosen men, carrying their spears point downward to the ground. Then ten sacred horses called Nisaian, richly caparisoned. (They are bred on the Nisaian plain in Media; hence their name; they are a tall breed.) Behind these ten horses was a chariot, sacred to Zeus, drawn by eight white horses, with the driver, reins in hand, following on foot—for no mortal might mount that seat. Then came Xerxes himself standing in a chariot drawn by Nisaian horses; his driver stood beside him, Patiramphes, son of Otanes, a Persian.

So Xerxes drove out from Sardis, and at intervals, if he was so minded, he would change from the chariot to a carriage. Behind him marched a thousand spearmen, carrying their spears in the usual manner, point upward, and then another select regiment of Persian horse; after the horse ten thousand men on foot, also selected men. Of these one thousand, half in front and half behind the rest, had golden pomegranates on their spear butts instead of spikes; the other nine thousand had silver pomegranates. (The spearmen who carried their spears point downward also had golden pomegranates, and those who followed immediately after Xerxes had gold apples.) After the ten thousand infantry came another ten thousand Persian cavalry; then a gap of two furlongs; *then* the rest of the army, all mingled together.

So they marched as far as Abydos on the Hellespont, passing Troy, which Xerxes felt impelled to visit, and when he had gazed upon it, he made a great sacrifice to Athena.

Is that a simple narrative of τί Ξέρξης ἔπραξεν, of what Xerxes did? Remember, besides this narrative, what we have been told of him and his expedition shortly before (vii 35): how, when the first bridge of boats across the Hellespont was destroyed, Xerxes on its being reported to him ordered the sea to be given three hundred lashes and that it be put in chains and even (so Herodotos had heard) *branded*, and these barbarous and reckless words to be uttered: "Thou bitter sea, thy master inflicts this punishment on thee for thy wrongs to him when he had done thee none. King Xerxes will cross over thee, whether thou likest it or no." Later (vii 44) when the great army was arrived at the Hellespont and had begun to cross, Xerxes, watching it from a white marble throne that had been specially erected for him, rejoiced when he saw all the straits full of *his* men, and congratulated himself; then began to cry. When his old counselor Artabanos, his uncle, asked him why this sudden change of mood, he answered: "It is the shortness of human life which saddens me. Not one of all these men will be alive in a hundred years."

Later still (vii 101–105) at Doriskos comes the talk[12] with Demaratos the Spartan; "how can the Greeks face my millions?" Demaratos tells Xerxes that the Spartans at least will fight, no matter what the numbers against them. "Are these countrymen of yours so mighty that each will fight ten Persians? At that rate you, their king, should be able to fight twenty. But this is idle boasting; even if five thousand of them assembled, we should still be a thousand to one. With a strong master, such as my army has, they might, for fear of him and of the lash, perchance fight above their nature and against great odds, but you say they are free. They would never do this." Demaratos answered that he knew that what he said would not please Xerxes, but he had been bidden to speak the truth. "It is no boasting. No one Spartan, and certainly not I, would challenge ten or even two men, but the *army* will stand its ground. We are free men, yet not altogether free, for over us is our law. This we fear more than your subjects fear you, and it

---

[12] I do not quote exactly, but rather provide the substance of the interchange.

forbids us to desert our allotted post." But Xerxes just laughed, and was in high good humor and not angry with Demaratos at all—this poor petulant sentimental fool of a prince.

This is not just narrative of things that happened, but Herodotos' philosophy, or rather (for he was no simpleton) one part of it. Prosperity as such is deceptive, a slippery thing; prosperity and power, accompanied by arrogance, by a contempt for the small size of the enemy, by a pride in the mere numbers of its own subjects and in the splendor of its autocratic rule—this is fatal and will fall. The narrative is not a statement of a particular event, but something generalized, καθόλου πεποιημένον, as generalized as Aeschylus' *Persai*; and the events related are *logically* connected, the one following the other κατὰ τὸ εἰκὸς ἢ τὸ ἀναγκαῖον, according to probable or necessary sequence, not ὡς ἕκαστόν τι ἐγένετο, as each thing happened, that is, in what Aristotle said was the manner of poetry and not the manner of history.[13]

It will be well to illustrate this argument by one or two examples from Herodotos, even though this means, in part, altering his narrative into a bald summary and thereby spoiling it, and, incidentally, making it difficult to follow. First, a very simple one from the early chapters (i 56–70). When Croesus, recking nothing of what Solon had said—for had he not mourned for his son two years, and was now consistently happy again and as rich as ever, ruling many contented subjects, by all of whom he was liked, and was not even the Delphic oracle behind him?—when he lightheartedly decided on war with Cyrus of Persia, with a good cause, naturally, for Astyages the Mede who had been recently overthrown by Cyrus was his brother-in-law, and besides it was necessary to attack Cyrus before he became too strong, he looked around for allies. He learned that Athens and Sparta were the leading Greek states, each belonging to a differ-

---

[13] Gudeman, in his note on *Poetics* 51b3 (p. 205), agrees that Herodotos was not a fortunate choice for Aristotle to have made, if he wanted to contrast poetry with history, because, he says, in Herodotos there is so much *märchenhaftes*. There is something in that, but it is not what is important.

ent section of the Greek race, the one Ionian and the other
Dorian. This gives Herodotos the occasion for a short digression
on the origin of the Ionians and Dorians, then to an account of
Athens at this time; she could not help Croesus, because she was
held in subjection by the tyrant Peisistratos, and we hear in
detail how Peisistratos had made himself, at the third attempt,
master of the city. Sparta, on the other hand, had just secured
the supremacy in the Peloponnese (which she still held a century
later in Herodotos' own day), and after a brief digression on her
early weakness and some account of her wars we hear that she
was ready to help Croesus. A last anecdote follows to explain a
particular indebtedness to him.

Herodotos was, naturally, not concerned to explain Greek
customs and institutions to his Greek readers, as he was to set
forth those of the many foreign races which made up the Persian empire, but he did want to give an account of the recent
history of the Greek states in order to explain their actions and
inactions in 490 and 480 B.C. And he does it by means of such
digressions, often very complex digressions, in his story of the
rise of the Persian Empire, wherever he can find, as it were, a
logical excuse for an "episode," as Aristotle would call it in an
epic, a digression which, again like an episode in a long poem,
helps also to give variety to the narrative and some relief to the
hearer or reader. So in the course of this episode of Croesus,
already thus early in the whole *History*, we get to know something of the two Greek states which are to play the leading part
in resistance to Persia, as well as something of Persia herself.

My second example is drawn from book iii 39 ff.; it interrupts
the story of Kambyses' campaigns in Egypt and from Egypt,
westward and southward. I choose it because, unlike my first,
it is of the complex type; it also is interesting because it *appears*
to have nothing but a chronological connection with the main
narrative; we seem to have something from "a chronicle, or
register, of events taken just as they come in order of time, however separate or disconnected they may have been in themselves." For it begins simply: "While Kambyses was preparing

for his campaigning against Egypt, Sparta made an expedition against Samos and its ruler, Polykrates." We are told how Polykrates became tyrant, after killing one brother and driving out the other, and prospered exceedingly, and made friends with Amasis, king of Egypt. (We see some connection with the main narrative here.) He was a great privateer, raiding everyone alike, friend or foe, saying that his friends were much more grateful to him for returning what he had stolen than they would have been had he never stolen at all. Amasis became alarmed at his friend's prosperity, and wrote to him thus: "I don't like your good fortune at all; know that the divine is always envious. I would much rather a friend of mine was successful only some-times, and at others failed; it is much safer. Try to do something about it." Polykrates was impressed with this sage philosophy, and there follows the story of how he tried to lose his precious ring, but failed. When he told Amasis of this, the latter broke off his friendship, sure that his ally would come to a bad end. This is the simplest example, the least alloyed, of the doctrine that prosperity is dangerous, which we have already had in a more subtle form in the story of Croesus.

It was against this Polykrates that Sparta was to send an expedition, urged on by Samian exiles driven out by Polykrates after the latter had tried to send them, his political enemies, with a force to help Kambyses in Egypt but with a secret re-quest that they be not allowed to return. (Again the *logical* contact.) They managed to get back, however, but were de-feated by Polykrates and came to Sparta for assistance. They made a long speech, to which the Spartan authorities replied that they had forgotten the first half and did not understand the second. Not to be put off or to be outdone, the orators brought in an empty sack and said: "The sack wants corn." There was no need to use the word "sack," say the Spartans (46.1). However, they promised help, not so much to gratify the exiles as to punish Samos for having stolen a bowl which they were sending Croesus a generation earlier. Corinth urged Sparta on in this, for they too had suffered an outrage at the hands of Samos. The outrage was of this nature. Samos had rescued three hundred boys, the sons of the first men in Ker-kyra, whom Corinth was sending to Lydia to be made eunuchs, and had prevented the Corinthian escort from recovering them.

The reason why these boys were being sent to Lydia was as follows: Periandros, tyrant of Corinth, had murdered his wife; he had had two sons by her, now eighteen and seventeen years of age. They went on a visit to their mother's father in near-by Epidauros, who told them how their mother had died. The elder took no heed of the story, but the younger, Lykophron, was so grieved that when he got home he refused to speak a word to his father or to answer a word addressed to him. At last Peri-andros, in a rage, drove him from the house, and pressed the elder brother to say what it was that they had heard from their grandfather that could so have affected the boy. In the end the elder brother recalled it and told him. Periandros understood, and, determined not to show any weakness, sent an order to those who were befriending Lykophron not to entertain him any longer. So Lykophron went from house to house, no one liking to refuse hospitality to the tyrant's son but all feeling under compulsion to obey the tyrant's decree to expel him. Finally Periandros issued an order imposing a large fine, to be paid to Apollo, on anyone who should receive his son or even speak to him. Whereupon the boy went to sleep in the marketplaces and lay about on the ground there. Three days later Periandros saw him lying there dirty and starving, and took pity on him: "Is this life here better than life with me in the palace, which you may have as my son? Do you, a prince of great Corinth, choose to live the life of a beggar by opposing and being bitter against me, your father? If you have some suspicion of me about a past misfortune, *I* have to bear the greater burden of that, not you. Remember that it is better to be envied than pitied, and wicked to live in anger against your father and your king; so return home." But the boy made no answer to him save that he, Peri-andros, must now pay a fine to Apollo for having spoken to him. So Periandros, seeing that the thing was hopeless and that there was nothing to be done, sent him to Kerkyra, which was within his dominion. Years passed and Periandros wished to leave his throne to Lykophron, considering his elder son little better than half-witted, and sent messengers to recall him to Corinth, but Lykophron would not even send an answer. Periandros then sent his daughter, Lykophron's sister, to persuade him, but nothing that she could say, of all the wise saws her father had taught her, could prevail on him except to elicit the statement that he would not return to Corinth while his father lived. The latter then sent a third time, to say that he would himself come to Kerkyra and live there if Lykophron would return to Corinth and succeed to the throne. At last Lykophron consented and preparations were being made to that end when the men of Kerkyra, ready to do anything rather than have Periandros among them, killed the prince. That is why Periandros took revenge on them and sent the three hundred boys to Lydia; hence also Corinth was at enmity with Samos for rescuing them and urged the Spartans to attack her.

Herodotos now returns to the Spartan expedition against Polykrates of Samos in aid of the Samian exiles; the first Spartan campaign in Asia, he adds, for their resolve to aid Croesus had come to nothing. He then in some detail narrates its failure and thereafter the subsequent fortunes of those Samians as freebooters and privateers in the Aegean till their final overthrow by Aigina, at enmity with Samos because of a bitter war of some two hundred years earlier. Concluding his digression, Herodotos says: "I have written thus at length about Samos because the island can show the three largest constructions in the Greek world: a tunnel cut through a mountain to bring water to the city, a mighty mole around the harbor, and the largest temple I have ever seen. To return to Kambyses in Egypt . . ."; and the main thread of the narrative is resumed.

In form, you observe, this is simply relating one event, the Spartan war against Samos, in company with another contemporary event, Kambyses' conquest of Egypt and his stay there; between these two there is but the thinnest possible connection

in Polykrates' abortive attempt to get rid of his enemies by
sending them to support the Persian; it is apparently an instance of a chronicle of events just taken in order as they
occurred. In fact, it contains one digression within another,
including the grim story of Periandros and his son; and if it is
not given a very good excuse other than its own interest, neither
is the Diomede-Glaukos episode in the *Iliad*. That also has a
weak motive and contains within itself an inner digression, the
story of Bellerophon, which has no organic connection with the
story of the *Iliad* except to illustrate the general life of the Greek
heroes, and, as I suggested above (p. 39), to help attune our
minds to the meeting of Hektor and Andromache in Troy.

Herodotos' method is, in fact, an elaboration of Homer's,
but because he is a historian, not a poet, he has something to do
besides tell the story; he is building up the history, or parts of
the history, of the Greek states in the two generations or so
before the Persian Wars, side by side with that of the growth
and nature of the Persian Empire. For example, he has more to
tell us elsewhere about the tyranny at Corinth, and in quite a
different context. He has arrived, halfway through his whole
book, at the beginning of the Ionian revolt, eight or nine years
before Marathon; Aristagoras of Miletos goes first to Sparta,
then to Athens, for help, to Athens not long before freed from
her tyrants—which happened as follows. We have an elaborate
series of stories within stories, of the tyranny at Athens and the
liberation of the city from it, of wars with Aigina, of how Sparta
helped to overthrow the Athenian tyrant but, on the subsequent
success of the democrats against the oligarchs of Athens, tried
in vain to support the latter, and at last decided, in order to
weaken Athens, to propose the forcible restoration of the tyrant.
Then Soklées of Corinth broke out: "Surely the world is upside
down, men will be living in the sea and fishes on the land, if
Sparta is to restore tyrannies in Greek cities. We in Corinth
know what tyranny is like. Kypselos was our tyrant, whose ill-
foreboding birth was told to us by the Delphic oracle; when the
child was born, the ruling families sent ten of their number to

its home to kill it." We expect another grim story like that of
Periandros; but "the baby's mother, suspecting nothing and
supposing this to be a visit of courtesy and friendship to her
husband, brought it out and handed it to one of the men; they
had previously arranged that the first to take the child should
dash it to the ground. But it smiled in his face and he could not,
in pity, kill it, and so handed it to the next man, who felt the
same about it, and handed it to the third, and he to the fourth,
and so on through all ten of them, and none could do it. So the
mother took the child from them indoors again, and'they fell to
upbraiding each other, and especially the first of them, and
decided to try again; but she overheard their talk and hid the
child, and they returned to the city and said that they had carried out their orders." So Kypselos grew up and became tyrant,
and was a bad man and oppressed the rich, although not quite
as much as his son Periandros did. "We therefore," says the
Corinthian, "are amazed that you Spartans should attempt to
restore a tyrant, and call upon you, by the gods of Greece, to do
no such thing, and if you do, you will get no support from
Corinth." Applause greeted this speech, and Sparta withdrew
her proposal, and with that, and a little more about the for-
saken ex-tyrant of Athens, Herodotos returns to the point where
he started, to the main thread of the history, the arrival of
Aristagoras at Athens, where he found a democracy established,
to ask for help for their kinsmen of Ionia against Persia, which
these foolish democrats granted.

Let me end this chapter by making the obvious comments on
Herodotos' method of narration. First, in these digressions, as
in his main narrative, he is not simply "recording events,"
whatever that may mean, but writing in the "poetic" manner
according to Aristotle's use of the word "poetic"; he is the most
gifted of storytellers. Secondly, we can criticize this last episode
because its motive is wrong in that Sokleës is intending to
frighten his audience by telling the horrors of tyranny, but for
half his speech engages our sympathies entirely with the child
and its mother, and not at all with the ruling oligarchs of

Corinth. This criticism, you will note, is of Herodotos as *artist:* that he tells the story entirely for its own sake, not as one that would be told by such a speaker as the Corinthian delegate on such an occasion, just as, if we like, we can say that it is not probable, ἐκ τῶν εἰκότων, that Glaukos told Diomede the longish story of Bellerophon in the middle of the battlefield. Thirdly, we may criticize Herodotos as *historian* for giving this speech of Sokleës just where he did, and for supposing so naïvely that it was this speech which turned the Spartans from their purpose; there is a lack of serious political thinking here. But fourthly, we can only wonder at and admire that *historical* gift of his, which I have in fact concealed by picking out two stories and greatly abbreviating the rest, characteristic though these stories are; that he can so wield his immense and varied material, the whole story of the Persian Empire and so much of the history of the many Greek states, that he can make it not only εὐσύνοπτον, comprehensible as an organic whole, but historically so significant as well.

This is all very unsatisfactory as an account of Herodotos' methods, but I will excuse myself on the ground that he more than most writers is one to read, not to talk about; he so clearly explains himself, at least if one allows oneself to read him without a mass of preconceptions. The next chapter should make the purpose of what I have been saying a good deal clearer.

V

Herodotos and Aeschylus

It may seem that all that I have done, or tried to do, is to prove what surely needs no proving, that Aristotle's treatment of history in the *Poetics*, interesting as it is, is yet inadequate; but that is not my purpose. Rather is it to use his comparison of history with poetry as a stimulus in the examination of the ways of Greek poet and historian in dealing with historical themes; there is obviously an essential difference between them, as Aristotle saw, but in what does it lie? Take another instance from Herodotos and on the basis of it compare him with Aeschylus. I have already commented on the fact that the *historian* must take note of the latter's account of Salamis, or at least of some statements in it such as those relating to the number of ships engaged, especially those on the Greek side; the false reports of Greek movements sent to Xerxes; the fighting on the small island in the straits; the high place from which Xerxes himself surveyed the fighting. All this may, from the historical point of view, be profitably compared with the account in Herodotos.

Further, for a picture of the Persian armada, as the Greeks saw it, we shall do well to read the opening chorus of the play with its fine list of the various troops in the king's army and their noble commanders, and how they crossed the Hellespont, as well as Herodotos' more elaborate description, both his detailed catalogue and the story of Xerxes' majestic march from Sardis which I quoted in chapter iv. But for my purpose there is a more significant passage from Aeschylus' story of the battle of Salamis itself. As day broke, the Persians—you will remember, of course, that the whole of the play is presented from the

95

Persian side and that there are no Greek characters in it—heard a great cry from the Greek camp, and it was not a cry of despair, as they had been led by the false message to expect, but of courage, and the signal for attack was given and the Greek ships advanced in good order. With that another call was heard:

> ὦ παῖδες Ἑλλήνων, ἴτε,
> ἐλευθεροῦτε πατρίδ᾽, ἐλευθεροῦτε δὲ
> παῖδας, γυναῖκας, θεῶν τε πατρῴων ἕδη,
> θήκας τε προγόνων· νῦν ὑπὲρ πάντων ἀγών.

$$(402-405)$$

That is magnificent poetry: "Come, sons of Greece: free our country, free our wives and children, the temples of our gods and the tombs of our fathers; now is the moment which will decide all"; but, if we are thinking of the story of the Persian Wars, of what does it remind us? Surely of the speech of Miltiades to Kallimachos in Herodotos before battle was engaged at Marathon (vi 109.3): ἐν σοὶ νῦν, Καλλίμαχε, ἐστὶ ἢ καταδουλῶσαι Ἀθήνας ἢ ἐλευθέρας ποιήσαντα, κ.τ.λ. It might at first suggest one of the speeches at Salamis, that of Themistokles to Eurybiades, which in part resembles that of Miltiades, ἐν σοὶ νῦν ἐστὶ σῶσαι τὴν Ἑλλάδα, but that is much tamer (viii 60); or the curiously rhetorical summary of Themistokles' address to his sailors (viii 83.1): τὰ δὲ ἔπεα ἦν πάντα τὰ κρέσσω τοῖς ἥττοσι ἀντιτιθέμενα, ὅσα δὴ ἐν ἀνθρώπου φύσι καὶ καταστάσι ἐγγίγνεται· παραινέσας δὲ τούτων τὰ κρέσσω αἱρέεσθαι καὶ καταπλέξας τὴν ῥῆσιν, ἐσβαίνειν ἐκέλευσε ἐς τὰς ναῦς, or the words of the ghostly spirit in the form of a woman which upbraided the Greeks for at first retreating before the Persian: ὦ δαιμόνιοι, μέχρι κόσου ἔτι πρύμνην ἀνακρούεσθε; (viii 84.2), which in spirit is more like Aeschylus. And there are other things too in Herodotos in his account of Salamis itself which are like this; but in dramatic power, in its aptness to its place in the story, it is Miltiades' speech which is most closely comparable. The Athenians are in their strong defensive position at Marathon, while the Persians, greatly outnumbering them (as Herodotos sees it, at least), face them near the shore. For days neither side moves and the Athenian generals are divided over whether to engage the enemy or no; Miltiades was urgent for battle:

It lies with you now, Kallimachos, either to bring Athens to slavery or, by making her free, to win a memory for all time such as not even Harmodios and Aristogeiton won. Athens has never been in such danger. If we yield to the Persian, we know the fate decreed for us, but if we gain the battle, she will be the first city in Greece. We generals are divided, but I am convinced that if we do not engage in battle, a serious strife of opinion will shake our resolve and make us take the Persian side; but if we engage, before rot sets in among certain groups in Athens, then, if the gods grant equal chances, we shall win. All this has now come to you, depends on you; if you take my side, our country will be free and our city the first in Greece; if you take the other, the very opposite of all this will befall us.

Kallimachos chooses right; he joins Miltiades, and Athens and Greece, with all that they stood for, were saved. With this great speech Herodotos achieves two aims: first (which does not concern us here), he makes clear why Miltiades and not Kallimachos was always regarded as the moral author of the victory in spite of the latter's position as polemarch, and his vote the decisive one, and his brave death in the battle; secondly, and this is what is important for us, he makes clear in a dramatic way the historic importance of the campaign and the Athenian victory—the tension of the moment, the hard-won adhesion of Kallimachos, who is persuaded only by such moving eloquence, and the subsequent battle. So does Aeschylus bring before us so well the tension of the moment at Salamis; νῦν ὑπὲρ πάντων ἀγών.

Of Aeschylus we ask no more, but of Herodotos, since he was a historian, we must ask much.[1] The first question is: how did he know the words used by Miltiades in private conclave with Kallimachos? This is not a pedantic question to be answered simply by saying: "My authorities tell me that the polemarch had to be won over before the decision to engage the enemy was

---

[1] I have discussed the historical implications of the speech at greater length in my paper on the Marathon campaign in *Phoenix* VI (1952), pp. 77–83.

made, and that the fear of the effect of delay on Athenian morale, or of a purely defensive attitude, was what decided the issue, and this I have expressed in direct rather than in indirect speech" (which has not the same meaning in Greek as it would have in English).[2] The whole manner of the speech is that of one made, actually made word for word as reported by one who knew; that is, it is in the manner of poet or novelist who does know the actual words used by his characters, of which and of the situations in which the speeches are made he is himself the creator, ποιητής. Another question, certainly of equal importance to the historian, is: were these arguments used on this occasion and to Kallimachos? Are they not rather, with their fear of civil strife and a weakening of morale, those that were used (by Miltiades) in the assembly at Athens before the decision was taken to march out to Marathon at all, when he made the proposal to march there as Aristotle says that he did (*Rhet.* iii 10, 11a11): "not only will our position at Marathon be strategically and tactically a strong one, but a bold decision will both shake the enemy and give ourselves courage in this time of mortal danger"? I am not suggesting that Herodotos deliberately altered the place of this speech in his history for the sake of dramatic effect, any more than he altered the year of the eclipse of the sun (above, p. 74) for a similar reason; that would be quite foreign to him, as I shall argue presently. I am only saying that we must ask of Herodotos questions that would be quite meaningless if put to Aeschylus about his narrative of a historical event, and that these questions shake his position as historian by suggesting that he has not taken sufficient care in testing his authorities, or in understanding what they told him, and that he is treating his material as a poet might. "Put Herodotos into verse," says Aristotle, "and he would remain a historian none the less, not a poet." But the speech of Miltiades at least would go admirably into verse; or rather, since Aristotle agrees that some ποίησις, that is, creative art, was in prose, this

---

[2] On the significance of direct and indirect speech in relation to the speeches in Thucydides, see my *Essays*, pp. 173–174.

speech *is* poetry in Aristotle's sense. He includes "Socratic dialogues" among his instances of creative art in prose; and we may recall the passage from the *Republic* which I referred to in an earlier chapter (above, p. 62), the one that ends Sokrates' discussion of epic and tragedy in his republic; it is a similar kind of "poetry": "Yes, Glaukon, for much is at stake, more than most people think"—μέγας γάρ, ἔφην, ὁ ἀγών, ὦ φίλε Γλαύκων, μέγας, οὐχ ὅσος δοκεῖ.

There is many a story in Herodotos which is poetry in this sense, the unforgettable one of Croesus and Adrestos, Kyme and the suppliant Paktyes, Periandros and Lykophron, in a lighter vein that of the birth and narrow escape from death in infancy of Kypselos of Corinth. Aristotle would have agreed, and might have answered us that these are but episodes with which he varies his narrative, just as Homer does, who, though he has singled out one section only of the whole Trojan War for his story, "brings in many of the other incidents as episodes, using the Catalogue of the Ships, for instance, and other episodes" [e.g., Achilles' sack of Thebe, Andromache's city] "to relieve the uniformity of his narrative" (23, 59a35). But though it is true that Herodotos, having decided to write a *history*, was not free to "single out one section only" of the Persian War, and his whole work is therefore not "poetry," whatever some episodes may be, yet this answer does not satisfy, and for two reasons. First, these "episodes" are not isolated. They are numerous and of the very fabric of Herodotos' history, now, like Croesus and Adrestos, helping to show the true meaning of the whole story, the real significance of the Persian defeat, now an episode in the complex narrative of events which he has succeeded in making into an organic whole, now in the very heart of the story. Aristotle praised Homer for not attempting to deal even with the Trojan War in its entirety, "though it was a whole with a definite beginning and end," through a feeling, apparently, that it was too long a story to be taken in in one view, or, if not that, too complicated from the variety of incident in it (59a34): a very just, if obvious, judgment; but it is interesting that he did not see, or at least did not say, that this is what Herodotos so successfully did, that he made the long and complicated story both one and εὐσύνοπτον, "capable of being taken in in one view." It might indeed have occurred to him that Herodotos was the more an artist, a ποιητής, because he thought that the "memorable deeds" should be recorded for their own sake, *as a complete story*, without that sense of the continuity of history which Thucydides so conspicuously possessed.

The other reason why such an answer (that *some* "episodes" in Herodotos may be "poetic") is inadequate is that in this sense the scene on the field of Marathon, Miltiades and Kallimachos in consultation, is not at all an "episode"; it is central to the whole story, part of its backbone, as much as, in its way, is the embassy to Achilles in the *Iliad*. So are the conversations between Xerxes and Artabanos before the great invasion was decided, and the debates between Greek generals on the very eve of battle. It is Herodotos' method to write in the "poetic" manner, as a creative artist, as we might express it; and while this is easiest to see in his speeches, which he always reports in the artist's manner, whether in a story of the past, like that of Kandaules and Gyges, or in the private discussions of contemporary persons, as Xerxes and Artabanos, about the war, yet he can adopt the same manner in his narrative, as for instance in his description of Xerxes' march from Sardis to the Hellespont. Once more, I do not mean that he altered what he believed to be true for the sake of dramatic effect, or that he allowed himself that little license which Bywater speaks of as the privilege of poets (πολλὰ ψεύδονται ἀοιδοί); on the contrary, I am sure he believed that Xerxes and his army did march in this manner from Sardis, and, for all we know, he may be right in this belief, just as every detail in Aeschylus' account of Salamis, numbers of ships and all, may be accurate; but for all that, both narratives are, in essentials, "poetic" and the authors are the "poets" of their story.

I wish to emphasize this because the difference between poetry and history is sometimes obscured. T. R. Glover, for example, in his Sather lectures on Herodotos of nearly thirty years back, which contain so much that is sensible, in discussing the story of Croesus and his captivity (above, p. 81), of which two versions are known, that in Herodotos and another according to which Croesus *was* burned to death by Cyrus, says that Herodotos, "with his historical principles, may be credited with not inventing for himself the version which he gives." So far, I am sure, Glover is right; but he goes on: "He may well have known the other version and preferred what he has given us, a tale more full of marvel, obviously, and not without a moral (more than one in fact), and, to rise to a higher plane of criticism, a tale more fragrant with wise and genial humanity. What reader but likes Cyrus and Croesus better, as he overhears their talks in the years of their consorting?" (p. 131). Glover did not see, apparently, that this is a criticism, an appreciation, of a storyteller, not of a historian. Or again on Herodotos' account of Egypt, which, though of such great value, yet has many errors, and gross errors, he writes (p. 135): "We have thus something that is really of far more interest and far higher value than exact information, given objectively, of Egypt about 450 B.C. We have the reaction on the general Greek mind, expressed by a man of singular sensitiveness, solid honesty and real sympathy," etc. This is to confuse two things, for we should equally have the reaction of Egypt on a Greek mind if Herodotos had written a novel about it.[3] Of course, if we wish to understand Greece of the mid-fifth century we must read Herodotos, as we must read Aeschylus and Sophokles, whether his history is in general accurate or not; but that does not free us from the necessity of inquiring into its accuracy and of criticizing inaccuracy when we find it as we would not criticize it in a poet or a novelist. If we want to understand mid-nineteenth-century England, we should read Macaulay as well as Tennyson and Dickens, but it does not follow that we are content to say, "What an excellent reflection of his own generation Macaulay

---

[3] See as well Glover, pp. 85–87, where he also writes as though history and fiction were the same thing.

gives," without asking any questions about the historical value of his history of the reign of William and Mary.

Nor should we treat Herodotos like a child and say that we must not apply twentieth-century standards to his work. Sometimes by this is meant no more than that he did not have card indexes, sometimes that he did not possess the knowledge that archaeology especially has given us, which is not much more important, sometimes even that he was debarred from footnotes, which is not even true, for he says that he had to have them constantly (iv 30.1). But we can, and should, demand from him honesty, intelligence, and diligence, which are not the prerogatives of our own age alone, and where he fails by a too ready acceptance of an account which is a good story for its own sake, or by an ignorance of politics and war, of course we must criticize, as Thucydides criticized him. What else can we do but judge by our own standards? The sense of value is part of history, and "the unfailing vitality" of the great writers that we talk about implies that the standard must be a living one. Certainly for Herodotos there is no need for kindness; in the end he comes triumphant from the test.

To return to Miltiades and Marathon. His speech is central in that by its means Herodotos makes clear the importance, that is, the historic and not simply the dramatic importance, of the campaign and of the Athenian victory. The victory foreshadowed that of 480–479, and subsequent events. It foreshadowed, first, the rise of Athens herself to be "the foremost city of Greece" and a formidable power, supreme at sea, in all the eastern Mediterranean, though Miltiades, in the speech, restricts himself to "the first city of Greece"; second, the victory of the Greeks generally over the Persians. Herodotos says that the Athenians were the first Greeks to face the Persians bravely in battle; before them the Greeks had been frightened at the very sight of a Persian army—a great exaggeration, as we know from his own history. But an understanding one, for not only was Marathon the first victory in set battle, but the subsequent victory was against all the odds, a well-nigh im-

possible victory of a small, poor, and hopelessly divided people
over a powerful and well-organized empire, still in full tide of
recent expansion and victory, so that the Greeks may well have
been frightened. Professor Kitto in his recent short study of the
Greeks, in the Penguin series, has well brought out the fortunate
circumstances in which the Greek states, as we know them,
came into being in the Aegean world, from the ninth to the
seventh century, fortunate because there was then no strong
power in Asia or Egypt, or in Europe, in Macedonia or Thrace,
either to oppose their settlements around the Aegean and later
in South Italy and Sicily, or to interfere with them in their early
years; no aggressive empire, and no state in Asia ready even to
claim the whole of the continental area as its own. They were
left free to expand, and then to establish themselves with, in
the East, the Aegean rather than peninsular Greece as their
center. It was, when you think of it, to the last degree improbable that a people of one blood, one speech, one religion, as they
did not cease to remind themselves, should divide into hundreds of little states with populations of thirty or forty thousand
each, jealous of their political independence, each ready to
defend itself in arms against its neighbor; that they should,
jointly, take over a system of writing from the Phoenicians and
make the first true alphabet, but each keep to its own way of
writing it; should borrow another fruitful invention, a coinage,
but each state issue its own, with its own device and differing
standards; that all should be tenacious of that common religion,
but that each should devise a separate calendar for its festivals—doing, that is, things, new things, in common as a single
people, but also doing them separately. As it happened, with
such happy results for the Greeks and so for the world, there
was none to interfere with them in the early centuries; they were
left free to quarrel among themselves, to develop agriculture,
manufacture, and trade, to try political experiments, to devote
long hours to philosophy, art, and letters; and thus to reach
their unalterable conviction that this was the life for them.
What was to be expected, happened: a power did arise to

threaten them. The Medes and Persians took over the old Mesopotamian empires, and spread their rule. With hardly more than a shrug of the shoulders they absorbed the flourishing, active Greek states in Asia Minor, and, being a tolerant people, left them to live as they would, so they kept the peace and paid some taxes. This Persian empire was well organized; the wise Darius is one of the great figures of history. Its further expansion began soon afterward; after a failure in Scythia, they moved westward against Europe; the Thracian tribes, Macedonia, and the Greeks of that seaboard, all succumbed. How could peninsular Greece hold out? Xerxes laughed the idea to scorn, and indeed it *was* absurd. Even if all the states there had been of one mind for resistance, even if all quarreling had been laid aside and a superhuman good-will had sprung up among them, yet an army composed of many small, separately trained units could hardly hold its own against a more numerous and, apparently at least, a better trained and organized force. And they were very far from unanimity; some states kept aloof, nursing old grudges; others hesitated, fearful of destruction; some went over to the enemy, eager for power. There were the expected jealousies and recriminations among those which were determined to resist, and not less jealousy among the individual commanders. But the miracle happened and they won decisively.

Neither in the moment of danger when the invading army was approaching, nor afterward in the light of the risk that had been run, did the Greeks think of changing their political system, that of the numerous separate states; they did not attempt a federal government, a single state, and imagine that they would be at once by so much the more efficient. Had the idea occurred to them, their answer would have been: "We do not want that kind of political life and we are fighting to defend the life we prefer, whatever our weaknesses; that is what the war is about." And, from another point of view: "We shall fight all the better if we fight in our own way in which we have been trained, not in another hastily learned."

There was another thing the Greeks were fighting for: within each state the rule of law, constitutional government as we should call it; whether oligarchic or democratic did not matter so long as law prevailed and not the will of an individual or a clique. They pictured the Eastern monarch as ruling by his own will, not constrained by a law which bound all, whether he was generous and kind like Croesus, wise like Darius, or was the mad Kambyses or the foolish Xerxes. They had had autocrats of their own in many states, and some of them had been wise and competent rulers, but they had got rid of them all and preferred the rule of law.

All this Herodotos understood very well. He did not know much about the management of public affairs, any more than he did about the movement of armies in battle, or before battle, and most of his accounts of politics and war are naïve, but he understood the essential truth, what was at stake, what the war was about. He does not minimize or conceal the weaknesses on the Greek side; on the contrary, all that we know and more than what we know of their jealous quarrels and incompetences comes from him. He could expressly praise Persia when she recovered the Greek cities of Asia after their revolt for the way she established peace among them, stopped their constant internecine warfare, and ruled them well. (True, they were Ionians, and he could think it good for them to be cared for like children.) But he was a Greek all right, like the others as glad as he was astonished that the war was won and the invader sent home; glad that by these unexpected victories their peculiar institutions had been saved, and that on the political side the small state, in which each citizen could take a direct part in government, and the rule of law would continue. It might be objected that it is Herodotos, Aeschylus, and other Greeks on whom we rely for this interpretation of the Persian Wars; that they have imposed their view on posterity, and that if we had the full Persian story we might think differently. The answer is that no such history on the Persian side was written. Official records, yes, and if we possessed them we might know the true numbers of Xerxes' army. Brief chronicles, yes, but exactly not the kind of history which the Greeks wrote. This is no accident. The Persians did not write like Herodotos and Aeschylus; they had not that aptitude and inclination to put themselves on record consciously and intellectually, and so with an understanding of what the difference between Persia and Greece was. Thus the interpretation of Aeschylus and Herodotos *is* right; one thing that the Greek victory decided was whether men would continue to think as Aeschylus and Herodotos thought, and act as Tellos or Themistokles or Leonidas, or Aeschylus himself and his brother, acted.

There is, further, something in Herodotos, an essential part of him, which it is difficult to define, yet should not be ignored. It is not an inconsistency, for that would interfere with our enjoyment of his work, and I suppose there is no book, not even Boswell, of which we can be more sure that at whatever place we begin reading, it will give us pleasure; not therefore an unevenness in his art, but a difficulty which in reading him we might not notice, but would think about it afterward—gaps like chasms on a hill journey which, perhaps, we pass by and only remember when we are home. His military understanding is really very defective; he does seem to think that an army of a million and a half men, with an equal number of camp followers, just starts from one place at the signal given, marches for so many days, and arrives at another, and that too in a mountainous and nearly roadless country, and that these hundreds of thousands actually fought with the few thousands of Leonidas at Thermopylai. Yet in two passages he shows that he understood the main strategical problems, the first (vii 47–49) on the Persian side, when Artabanos warns Xerxes, himself excited only by the great size of his army, of the difficulties of supply, sure to increase the further they went into Greece (so Aeschylus too, *Persai* 790–794); the second from the Greek side, where he gives his judgment about the war, "a judgment which will not be popular" (vii 139). Athens, he says, by providing the largest number of ships and the best naval commanders and by the inspiring courage and endurance of all her citizens in the Salamis campaign, was chiefly responsible for the victory at sea, and it was this which made the over-all victory possible. It is not that he does not, here as elsewhere, give due praise to the Spartan hoplite who fought the bravest at Thermopylai and made the victory at Plataia (as Aeschylus again, "the victory of the *Dorian* spear," 817), and Persia was primarily a land power; but without Salamis, he says, Leonidas' death would have been in vain, for there would have been no Plataia. There might have been a second Thermopylai, but no victory. Most men, Herodotos implies, simply praise Sparta; but Athens, had she so chosen, *and she was sorely tempted*, could have spoiled everything. So that, in spite of all, he did understand the strategy of the war.

Secondly, when he describes politics in the narrower sense, and the political causes of events, he gives the motives of individuals for all they are worth, generally indeed private motives, which certainly are often inadequate to the events themselves. We cannot really believe that Corinth urged Sparta to her campaign against Polykrates of Samos about 525 B.C. solely because of the Samians' action fifty years before, which occurred as the result of a private quarrel between Periandros and his son, especially if we reflect that the political conditions in both states had changed since that time, the tyranny having been overthrown at Corinth and Polykrates' own having been established at Samos. The Ionian revolt was caused not alone by the desire of Histiaios to get away from the Persian court. Even if, as is probable enough, the exile of king Demaratos from Sparta was maneuvered for personal reasons by his enemies, and illegitimacy was the reason put forward by them, still it was a graver matter than one would suppose from Herodotos' way of telling the original story: how king Ariston had no children by his first two wives and so married a third time (incidentally by tricking his greatest friend), and she in less than nine months gave birth to Demaratos, and the news was brought by a servant to Ariston as he sat in council with the ephors. Recalling, says Herodotos, when he had married her and counting the months on his fingers, he exclaimed with an oath: "The child cannot be mine." He regretted that afterward and brought up Demaratos as his own son and was succeeded by him till the envious Kleomenes, aided by some of the ephors who, so many years later, remembered what Ariston had first said about his child's birth, got Demaratos deposed. That is not good political history as it purports to be. Yet, as I have just said, Herodotos had a profound understanding of what the war was about; what it was that made the difference between Greece and Persia, and what the Greek victory meant: the one disunited and fragmentary, the states numerous and small, exclusive, governed by amateurs, the citizens free, subject only to their own laws; Persia enormous by comparison, comprehensive and multifarious, tolerant, ruled by a governing class which had been trained in the art. It is in the mouth of this same Demaratos that he puts some of the best expression of this understanding.

That is what the victory meant for Greece and so for all western Europe. But humanity is wider than Greece, and Aeschylus, who was a patriotic Greek like Herodotos and saw what the victory meant, politically, for Greece, and says so in his play (vv. 213–214, 241–245), saw also that it had a wider significance for all men; the Persians were defeated because power corrupts, because great dominion breeds a desire for yet greater, and because success and prosperity are dangerous except for the wisest heads (as perhaps for Darius) and lead not only to an unthinking optimism, such as Croesus had, but to braggart boasting and insolent action that *must*, sooner or later (have we not seen it time and again?), bring disaster. This will happen to all men, quite independent of Greek or Persian. Herodotos understood that too, as Aeschylus did, and this philosophy pervades his *History*; but here again there is, it seems to me, in some way a contradiction. I do not mean by this that Herodotos often speaks of fate as though men's actions were impersonally determined, so that they were not responsible and could not be *guilty* of *hubris*—in the story of Croesus, for example, when, after the fall of his country, he upbraids the god of Delphi for the false oracles he had given to one who had been so generous with his gifts, and Apollo replies that not even a god can avoid fate, and it was fated that in the fifth generation after Gyges, who had killed his king Kandaules and usurped his throne, his successor should pay the penalty. To emphasize this by the exception that proves the rule, Apollo adds that in gratitude to Croesus he had tried to get the fates to postpone the fall of Lydia till after Croesus' death, and had got them to postpone it for three years but could do no more. Yet in no story does Herodotos make it more clear that a man is responsible for his own actions; that Croesus, because he was prosperous, was unthinkingly optimistic, was sure he would win, and light-heartedly undertook the war with Persia, and for that reason did not take the trouble to inquire further what the oracle meant; for Croesus admits that that was just the mistake that he made—he learned Solon's wisdom too late. Or take the earlier event, the tale of Gyges, the first in the book. Kandaules' wife says to him: νῦν τοι δυοῖν ὁδῶν παρεουσέων, Γύγη, δίδωμι αἵρεσιν ὁκοτέρην βούλεαι τραπέσθαι: "Gyges, I offer you the choice between two ways; take which you will" (i 11.2); here free-will is clearly implied in words that might have suggested Aristotle's explanation of character in a play (see pp. 65 f.), and that too though *necessity* is mentioned immediately after (i 11.4), which does not mean that Gyges had not power to choose. I do not understand how J. E. Powell can talk of "fatalism" as Herodotos' "philosophy of history," which has therefore "no ultimate moral significance."[4] There is, in fact, no possible story ("poetic" story) about human beings which does not imply free-will. A dramatist or novelist, or any other storyteller, may believe in determinism or fatalism in the abstract, but he must give his characters free-will, or they will be without interest; they must have a choice, as Herodotos knew by instinct even if he muddled his philosophy, and as Aristotle explained so clearly.[5]

---

[4] Powell, *Translation of Herodotus* (Oxford, 1946), p. xx.

[5] See I. M. Linforth, "Religion and Drama in Oedipus Coloneus," in *Univ. Calif. Publ. Class. Philol.* XIV (1951), pp. 91 and 146.

But if there is a confusion here when Croesus' fate is both ordained five generations back and brought about by his own thoughtlessness, that will be, I think, a case of what Professor Dodds has called in his recent Sather lectures "double determination," which is so frequently found in Homer (Achilles was "fated to die young," but that does not mean that he was not responsible for his actions);[6] at most it means that Herodotos was a historian, not an analytical philosopher. The sort of contradiction, however, which I had in mind lies rather in his skeptical and humorous attitude toward human affairs, in this so unlike Aeschylus, as though he were not really serious about either fate or human will. He tells, at the very beginning of the whole book, the story of Kandaules (another who, in but a few words, is depicted as the prince *delighted*, like Croesus and Xerxes, with his good fortune: he has the most beautiful of women as his wife), but he tells it as a *lighthearted* story. (If the newly found fragment of a play with this plot is, as it seems to be, from a tragedy, it must have been written in a very different spirit from that seen in Herodotos.) Kypselos of Corinth may have been a dread tyrant and his story may help to point one of the lessons of history, but the account of his birth is a humorous little tale; so is that of Demaratos, though Herodotos later puts in his mouth the political moral of the whole book. He has other stories that are tragic or grim, and his account of the folly of Xerxes is as eloquent (though so much more varied) as that of Aeschylus. Why in fact did Aristotle, when he was contrasting the austerity and the greater concentration of tragedy with the much greater length and variety of epic (26, 62b1 ff.; cf. 23, 59a30), not think also of comparing Aeschylus with Herodotos? He might have added something of value to what he says about history. Herodotos has every kind of story in his book, from the grimmest to the most gay. He was indeed a man of varied genius with an unceasing interest in the ways of mankind.

It is this universal interest which is the source of Herodotos'

---

[6] *The Greeks and the Irrational*, Sather Lectures XXV (1951), pp. 31-34.

impartiality, about which I would say a word, as I did on Homer. His was not the impartiality of the indifferent or of the man who puts himself above or aloof from his fellows, nor that of the austere judge who strips himself of his personal interests, but of the humanist. He was a Greek, and as glad of the victory as any of his countrymen, but his story is not one of gallant Greeks defeating an aggressive and barbarous enemy; indeed, for all that his book with its variegated theme was made *one* by his art, it is correct to say that the story of the victory is but half of it. The earthquake at Delos in 490 which was thought to be a portent, was certainly one, says Herodotos (vi 98.2), but it foreshadowed not the glorious victory over Xerxes ten years later, but the half-century of evils for Greece, caused partly by the Persians, partly by the subsequent wars among the Greek states themselves, struggling for primacy. The small squadron that Athens sent to help the Ionians in their revolt was not "the first step taken in the patriotic and victorious war," but the beginning of evil for Greek and foreigner alike (v 97.3), a statement that has worried many a modern scholar with narrower sympathies than Herodotos had. There were some in antiquity who said he was φιλοβάρβαρος, "on the side of the foreigner"; certainly Darius is the greatest man in his book, as Aeschylus too makes him a wise and good king. He was partial toward Athens and toward the Athenian democracy? He certainly praises the democracy when, after recounting their victories over Boeotians and Chalkidians, he notes that while they had been, in the time of the tyranny, in no way superior to their neighbors, now that they were free, they were better than all of them (v 78); but it was these same Athenians who, a year or two later, began the troubles of the world by sending, foolishly persuaded by Aristagoras, that fatal squadron to Ionia. He was partial to the Alkmeonidai? He certainly praised their resistance to the tyranny, and would not believe for a moment that they were responsible for the shield shown to the enemy at Marathon; very likely he did not see all the evidence, and did not make sufficient examination of what he had seen (so different a method from our own scientific procedure which, on the basis of the same evidence, builds a whole new structure of events); but that does not prove partiality, and immediately after his defense of their conduct at Marathon he tells the story of the origin of their wealth, the visit of Alkmeon to Croesus, which gently directs at them the most destructive of all weapons, ridicule. Glover mentions his admiration for Kimon and Perikles, "each of whom is brought into the history with an entry well prepared" (p. 32; Hdt. vi 136.3 and 131.2); but we should at least note that at the "entry well prepared" for Kimon, namely, the trial and condemnation of his father Miltiades, his great enemy was Xanthippos, father to Perikles. Whose side was he on? You cannot pin him down, and even Glover's words, mild and unobjectionable as they seem, are wrongly colored. He gives many partial reports from others which he did not sufficiently examine. He is fond of mocking the Ionian Greeks of Asia Minor, and in mocking them he conceals more than once the no better conduct of the Dorian states to the south, including his own city of Halikarnassos. But here too, though he perhaps disliked the Ionian influences in Halikarnassos and stresses the Dorian origin of the city (vii 99.3), he can tell a story not to its credit (i 144). Tyrants, it is said, he did not like, but in many he was interested and in their deeds: in Polykrates of Samos and others. All foreigners he found interesting. Egypt impressed him profoundly. The Persians he greatly admired, and of all the many individuals in his history, Darius, for wisdom, capacity, and generosity, comes out the best. Herodotos did not, we all agree, sufficiently test what he was told; and he will sometimes give a story for its own sake which he does not believe to be true. But he then says so. I do not therefore think that he either invented or consciously dramatized his history; I feel sure that he had heard that Miltiades' advice to Kallimachos was given on the field at Marathon and not some days previously in the assembly at Athens, and that he did not know two different stories about the end of Croesus and deliberately use the one that was more affecting or more dramatic.

It will help, I think, if I conclude this lecture with a more detailed analysis of one instance of what has been called Herodotos' partiality, his attitude toward Samos and the Ionians of Asia Minor. He was much interested in the island (see pp. 89–91), and stayed some time there. Modern scholars assure us that he was partial to the aristocracy that ruled it till they attempted to secede from the Athenian empire and were defeated in 439, and they will add that this in part explains the way in which he tells the story of the Ionian revolt against Persia in the nineties. For him the revolt was a mistake; the Athenians were foolish to help their kinsmen and fellow countrymen; the Persians were bound to win, and in fact when they did win they behaved sensibly and generously. Before the last battle, the naval fight off Lade near Miletos, the Persians, Herodotos tells us, were doubtful of winning, and sent the ex-tyrants of the Ionian cities opposed to them to each contingent, separately and unknown to the rest, to induce them to desert, with the usual promise of autonomy and prosperity if they did and with equally dire threats if they did not. But none would; they were obstinate, without judgment (vi 10: ἀγνωμοσύνῃ διεχρέωντο, a strong expression). Then Dionysios, from Phokaia, a small state whose contingent was only three ships out of three hundred and fifty-three, persuaded the others to put in some exercise and to practice maneuvers for the coming battle. They did so and went hard at it for seven days, but then the majority grumbled. They said to each other: "What crime have we committed that we are punished so? Have we gone completely out of our wits that we hand ourselves over, body and soul, to this man of Phokaia, which has only three ships? this man who inflicts on us pains incurable, so that many have already fallen sick and others are like to follow them? Rather than this let us be defeated if we must, and suffer whatever evils may befall us." So they refused to obey any longer, but stayed on land, put up tents, and sat about in the shade. The Samians, whose contingent was sixty ships, seeing what was going on among the Ionians—so Herodotos expresses it (13.1), as though the Samians were not Ionians,—recall the offer of their ex-tyrant, and determine, since "the Ionians" will not behave, that no victory is possible and that they had better decamp and so save their island, even at the expense of having their tyrant back.

The account of the battle then begins, and Herodotos says that he cannot say anything certain about who was brave and who cowardly, "for they blame one another." So far the narrative seems fairly clear: Herodotos is contemptuous of the Ionians and finds an excuse for the desertion of the Samians to whom he is so partial. But he goes on: when the battle was joined, the Samians, who were on the extreme right of the line, to the west, away from the land, sailed away, so it is said, all but eleven of them, and the Lesbians and "most of the Ionians" (14.3) followed suit. But the Chians, with the largest contingent of ships, one hundred in all, stayed and fought bravely and well, with very heavy losses, till they were overwhelmed, and this, in Herodotos, is no longer "obstinate folly," but an example of courage which deserves and gets full praise. So does the action of the eleven Samian captains who stayed, disobeying the order to desert. Moreover, in Samos itself a monument was set up to these eleven and their crews in memory of their courage, and Herodotos saw it there. Later, we are told (22.1), the men of substance in Samos, that is, *ex hypothesi*, Herodotos' friends, were ill pleased with what the other commanders had done in deserting at the battle, and would not wait for the tyrant's return, but set off to found a new colony in Sicily, where they behaved as badly as those freebooting Samian oligarchs who had been driven out by Polykrates a generation earlier. On whose side is Herodotos?

Come down to a yet later period and the picture is no clearer. The Samians and their governing class, around the middle of the century, were especially dear to Herodotos; he spent much of his time there; anyone will tell you that. It was this same people who seceded and were defeated by Athens, under the personal command of Perikles, in 440–439, and, equally, of course, Herodotos was partial to Athens and to Perikles. On whose side was he? In the particular matter of the Ionian revolt it is reasonable to say not only that Herodotos did not adequately examine what he was told, but that he did not form in his own mind a consistent picture of what happened. This last is a criticism of the artist as well as of the historian; but when a scholar wishes to show that Herodotos was partial to this or that city or group, he should always read the next sentence first: it may prove him wrong, even if he has not the imagination to understand what the historian was about.[7] It may also prove, occasionally, that Herodotos was careless, normally, that he was wise.

---

[7] Cornford, *The Unwritten Philosophy*, p. 15.

VI

Thucydides

Professor Wade-Gery in an interesting paper on Hesiod says, with special reference to the *Theogony* and the message of the Muses to the poet to tell the truth in his verses: "Hesiod did conceive of himself as a scientist rather than an entertainer: there is sense in calling him the first of the Pre-Socratics—the first of those scientists (or philosophers) who tried on the one hand to fathom the universe, on the other to advance some special technique. In all this his reaction from Homer is not unlike Thucydides' reaction from Herodotos."[1] This is a stimulating remark and one which we can accept—that is, for my purpose, just now, what in it relates to Thucydides. I am not one of those who think that Thucydides was frequently and purposely contrasting his theme and his treatment of it with Herodotos' theme and *his* treatment, or was scornful of him; on the contrary, where they overlap, he generally agrees, and he paid him the compliment that later historians were to pay to himself of beginning where he left off, not attempting to do again what he had once done, whereas he must do again what Hellanikos had attempted. But when he says that he himself took particular care to test information that he got from others, to allow for bias and for variation of memory, he surely has Herodotos in mind, who too readily accepted what was told him provided that it seemed "true" to the characters or to the event, for example, the talk between Solon and Croesus, so characteristic of the citizen of the Greek city and of the Eastern king, and so true to the subsequent story not only of Croesus but of Xerxes and his Persians and of mankind in general; or

---
[1] *Phoenix* III (1949), p. 86.

the speech of Miltiades to Kallimachos on the field of Marathon, so "true" to the speaker and to the significance of the battle, though neither, probably, is historically true—that is, Herodotos is thinking as a poet thinks, as Aeschylus thought, as a storyteller rather than as a historian. And when Thucydides adds that his work will be less attractive because it has nothing of τὸ μυθῶδες in it, he is still thinking of the storytelling element in his predecessor, not of the mythical in the sense in which we generally use the word, i.e., of the long past about which certainty is unobtainable; in fact, about that, Herodotos was much more skeptical and less serious than Thucydides, throwing doubt on the story of Helen of Troy (ii 113–120)[2] and on the very existence of Minos, though he can relate something of his history elsewhere (iii 122.2; i 171–173; vii 169–171), whereas Thucydides accepted them and rationalized their legends in the terms of fifth-century history, in the manner of the scientific historians of the nineteenth century A.D. By τὸ μυθῶδες Thucydides means those stories which Herodotos loved to tell both about the past (e.g., Kandaules and Gyges, or the birth of Cyrus or of Kypselos, Rhampsinitos and the clever thief) and about his own contemporaries (Xerxes and his dreams, or Xerxes and the storm at sea when he was returning to Asia), some of which he does not himself believe to be true and gives his reasons why. Such things Thucydides rejects in the interests of truth, and we say that Herodotos was after all an artist, while Thucydides was the first scientific historian. Which of the two then is σπουδαιότερος καὶ φιλοσοφώτερος, "of graver import and more philosophical," and thereby, for Aristotle, nearer to the poet, further from the pure historian? Apparently Herodotos; yet in one sense at least we should all agree that Thucydides was the more philosophical in his understanding of politics, and we should expect Aristotle, who was, among many other things, a political philosopher, to have recognized this.

When it is said that Thucydides was more scientific than

---

[2] By what Bywater would call "the little license allowed to the poet," Herodotos plays with the idea that Helen never went to Troy.

Herodotos and the first scientific historian, it is supposed at once, is it not, that he was on that account less an artist? For example, Professor Laistner in his Sather lectures of six years ago on the Roman historians said: "To the Greeks as to the Romans, a *History*, as distinct from a mere chronicle, was always an artistic product"; and some modern writers "have failed to understand that to all the ancients, even to Thucydides, a certain literary form and excellence were an integral part of historical composition." Again: Livy does not directly quote official documents; this was because "to have done so would have been to offend against the artistic canons of antiquity which required that the style of the *History* should be uniform and not marred by the introduction of official decrees, laws, and similar material. And even Thucydides generally conformed to this practice."[3] Why "even" Thucydides? Because he was so scientific, or because he was a lesser artist? Or does the one imply the other? The question is an interesting one.

I believe that this way of viewing the contrast between Herodotos and Thucydides is due to an unconscious belief that the artist, at any rate the artist whose task it is to write history, is in some way an amateur, a happy man who writes easily, who does not take much trouble, who "takes up" a thing almost as a hobby, and would not have to work too hard at it. This is what seems often the attitude of Roman writers; at least, I quote this further passage from Professor Laistner, who gives (p. 106) an extract from a letter of the younger Pliny. After explaining

---

[3] *The Greater Roman Historians*, Sather Lectures XXI (1947), pp. 8, 22, 86. Professor Laistner has a note to this last passage on p. 174 of his volume as follows: "The introduction of a treaty text in book v and of the agreement between Sparta and Persia in book viii has been used, in consequence, as an argument that Thucydides did not revise these sections before publication." It has, and a nice argument in a circle it is. Laistner forgets as well that there are three documents quoted *verbatim* in the section of the *History* which was completed, if any section was (which, of course, is by no means certain), namely, the treaties of iv 118–119, v 18–19, and v 23–24, besides the one he refers to (v 47); and there are two others in book v (77 and 79, in Doric) and three in book viii (18, 37, 58), not one. Further, Thucydides could quote Homeric hymns (also in another dialect) and epigrams on stone (iii 104; vi 54.7, 59.3). And how different *in style* from the documents quoted *verbatim* is such a one as that given in indirect speech in ii 24 or iv 16?

at length that he is too busy at the moment with legal work in the courts to think of historical writing, Pliny goes on as follows:

However, do you now reflect on this, on what period am I to begin? Former times, which others have described? The research in that case has been done, but comparing the various histories will be heavy work. Recent times, which no one has touched? This would cause offense to many and please few; for, in addition to the circumstance that in a very vicious age there must be far more to blame than to praise, you will be called niggardly of approval if you praise, too severe if you censure; and that, although you have done the former lavishly, the latter with the greatest restraint.

What a different world this is from the Greek! "If I decide to take up history, what shall I write about?" and this anxiety about praise and blame, and what the public will think of it! Not at all unlike the eighteenth century in England and France, and the attitude of even the greatest of historians, as Gibbon, but it is all quite foreign to Greece of the fifth century b.c. And we in consequence judge the Greeks by different standards, not only their art and their science but their politics too; we can and do judge them by the highest we know, and it is this which brings them so close to us.

In truth it is the artist, if a genuine artist as the Greeks were, who is the hard, plodding worker, who has to do everything for himself; if a painter, from the first sketches to the final touch of the brush on the canvas; if a writer of history, from the discovery of the facts to the last word and the last comma in their presentation. Thucydides in particular was, as Gilbert Murray said of him in his early work on *Greek Literature*, determined to do all the work himself and to present only the finished product to the public, as the artist does. Wren showed St. Paul's Cathedral to the world, not his plans for it; so does the painter his pictures, so did Pheidias his sculpture. Sometimes we are fortunate enough to possess the plans and the early designs and the sketches of details; and fascinating they are, not only for their own sake as drawings but also for the light they throw on

the master's method of work. It would be above all of interest
if we had the "notes" for his work which we know that Thucydides made, not only because we should learn much of his
method as a writer, but we should be in a better position to test
his credibility. Not his honesty (of that we are certain as we
are of Herodotos'), but his thoroughness as a historian. Herodotos is in this respect, more than Thucydides, what we so superficially call scientific; he often reveals his notes, tells us where
he has been, and what he has seen for himself, who his inform-
ants were, and how, to test some statement, "I went to Tyre,
and then to Thasos, and made inquiries of the people there."
That is more than Thucydides does; we know where he was on
only two occasions: he was in Athens during the great pestilence,
and he was in command in Thrace in 424; otherwise we only
know that he was never in two places at once, and that he was
not in Athens nor with any Athenian forces between 424 and
the end of the war twenty years later, and that he took advantage of his exile to be in touch with other sources, and especially
enemy sources, for the purposes of his history. Herodotos in
fact, as I said, uses footnotes, which *we* think at once establishes
a book as learned; Thucydides does not. But then, some, a very
few, modern scholars do not either. In the sympathetic memoir
of F. M. Cornford written as a preface to *The Unwritten Philosophy*, after stressing the great amount of reading that Cornford had to do in subjects outside his own field, Professor
Guthrie says (p. xvii): "Those of us who knew Cornford at that
time can only marvel at the completeness with which all this in
itself indigestible material was assimilated and transmuted, so
that the reader who is presented with the finished commentary
can scarcely be aware of the amount of patient labour that has
gone to its composition." Yet no one has doubted Cornford's
learning or the scientific quality of his work, even when we have
differed about his results; and in fact, in this sense, art and
learning, art and science, are not enemies, as I hope to show for
Thucydides.

This is all the more remarkable in him because he was doing

what hardly any other man has attempted—writing a strictly contemporary history. I am choosing my words carefully. Mr. Winston Churchill, as you have perhaps noticed, is a wise man; he says in the preface to his *Second World War*, Vol. I, that he had at his disposal many thousands of documents, largely from his own hand, which give a *current* account of events. "I doubt," he goes on, "whether any similar record exists or has ever existed of the day-to-day conduct of war and administration. I do not describe it as history, for that belongs to another generation. But I claim with confidence that it is a contribution to history which will be of service in the future." How wise that is: not history, but documents for history. But Thucydides did both; he collected all the material and wrote the completed history. He had one advantage over Mr. Churchill in that, though like him he began as an active participant in the war, with an important command, he was exiled, and Mr. Churchill has not been. He was thereby, as he says, given the opportunity of collecting material from both sides, and particularly from the enemy, and could observe events καθ' ἡσυχίαν μᾶλλον (v 26.5), which means not only "more at leisure" because he was not actively engaged in other work, but also with more peace of mind, so far as we can use the words "peace of mind" at all of Thucydides. His history was only intended to be complete for what he conceived to be his task: he was writing not a history of Greece, political, social, economic, and cultural during these years, but a history of the war, but it proved in fact, for the period which he lived to do, to be final. No one attempted to do again what he had done; the others began where he left off. Such official documents of the time as survive for us to study fill some gaps in the story, one or two of them important gaps, but in the main confirm it. The one other important evidence for the thought and feeling of the time, contemporary evidence from one of a very different temper from Thucydides, the comedy of Aristophanes, serves admirably to confirm and supplement his history. One historian of the enemy side who, as a boy, went through the siege of Syracuse within the city, which

Thucydides relates from without, from the Athenian side, could (so we are told; his work is lost) add little or nothing to what he wrote. Modern scholars can only translate or abridge. His triumph has been complete. And as a finished account of a strictly contemporary event his history must be almost unique. In this connection consider Aristotle's dictum once more. Aeschylus' *Persai*, a great tragedy about a contemporary event, must also be unique. It is clearly "philosophic" in Aristotle's sense, and a very notable instance of Aristotle's theory; but when we say that Thucydides' *History* is unique, or nearly unique, are we not saying much the same about it as about the *Persai?* That is, it is unique, as contemporary history, because it is not the materials for a history, but the finished product; but is it true that it would tell us simply "what Athens, Sparta, and the rest, did and suffered," whereas the tragedy is "more philosophic and of graver import"?

It will be well first to clear away a misconception, or to discuss expressions which may give rise to misconceptions. Thus Laistner, for example, minimizing the contrast between the later sensation-loving Greek historians (as they have been declared to be) and those of the fifth and fourth centuries, says (p. 14): "It is no new discovery in the Hellenistic age that the recording of human affairs offers opportunity for displaying situations of an intensely dramatic or epic character. There are plenty of episodes dramatically told in the pages of Herodotos. It is assuredly no accident that the Melian dialogue, the bluntest expression of Athenian imperialism, is immediately followed in Thucydides' *History* by an account of the Sicilian expedition." What are we to understand by this? Simply that Thucydides was *conscious* that his account of the conquest and cruel treatment of Melos, including the conference between Melian and Athenian delegates (called the "Melian dialogue," in which is discovered the altogether cynical attitude of the Athenians), preceded immediately the account of the Sicilian expedition? and that the cynicism of the former and the boundless and aggressive optimism of the latter make a pair and are in dramatic contrast to the disaster which overtook them? Of course he was; but this means only that he was writing intelligently. What else was he to do? The attack on Melos did precede almost immediately the planning of the expedition to Syracuse. Was Thucydides to put his events in the wrong order, or play down one of these two events, or insert some irrelevant twiddly bits (he does, indeed, insert some small events that were happening just then: v 115.1–3, 116.1) in order to avoid a dramatic contrast that was there in the events themselves? In fact, other such contrasts are to be found in Thucydides, one of them at least even more "dramatic," that between the idealism of the happy and confident Athens of the Funeral Speech at the end of the first year of the war, and the account of the pestilence which immediately followed, of the details of the disease and its ravages and the demoralization which soon accompanied it. Thucydides might have suppressed both the Funeral Speech and the Melian "dialogue"; would the result have been a more accurate history? Do we learn more from book viii, which has no speeches, than from the rest?

In book iii we have a different kind of contrast, the story of the secession of Mytilene from Athens and the war following, the fall of Mytilene and the savage resolution to kill all the men and sell the women and children into slavery (it was no more savage than the later treatment of Skione and Melos, but what was thought an atrocity at the beginning of the fighting was accepted afterward as a custom of war), the quick change of heart in Athens, and the countermanding of the resolution so that Mytilene was just saved because the first boat rowed slowly on its inhuman errand and the second fast and without pause for rest in order to arrive in time. Almost immediately afterward, Plataia, with only half its garrison left, reduced to complete helplessness after a long siege, surrendered to the Spartans. The Spartans had been particularly anxious that Plataia should surrender, not be captured by storm, so that in any subsequent peace negotiations on the basis of mutual restoration of conquests they could claim that it had joined them by agree-

ment, almost willingly, and therefore there would be no question of restoring it to Athens, or rather to the Plataian majority
that had taken refuge in Athens. Having secured this, they
went on to put every one of their prisoners on trial, putting to
them this one question: had they done any good service to
Sparta or her allies during this war? The Plataians made an
eloquent and moving plea, the Thebans (their special enemy, for
Plataia was Boeotian but refused to join the Boeotian federa-
tion, preferring an alliance with Athens across the border) a
hateful answer, in both of which we are reminded that whereas
Thebes had gone over to the enemy during the Persian Wars of
fifty years before, Plataia, a small place, had played a gallant ·
part, and her territory was the scene of the final, the liberating
victory of the Greek forces under Pausanias the Spartan, and
had been declared inviolable by all the Greek states thereafter.
To no effect; the Plataian prisoners, and some Athenians with
them, were condemned and put to death.

This follows the campaign of Mytilene, with its speech by
the Mytileneans asking for Peloponnesian help, and the great
debate at Athens between the advocates of rigorous treatment
and the moderates. Do you condemn Athens, silently asks Thucydides, as unworthy to rule over other cities? This, he says,
pointing to the enemy's treatment of Plataia, was the alterna-
tive, the way the Peloponnesians, the self-proclaimed liberators
of Greece, behaved. This is what war is like. He puts the question, as I said, silently, without comment: first Athens and
Mytilene, then Sparta and Plataia. He tells us just what happened; but he knew what he was saying, and it is by the speeches
he reports (or makes up, whichever you will) that he gives what
he regards as the proper emphasis to these events, that is, the
historical significance of events which from the purely military
point of view were interesting indeed (for, amongst other things,
the one showed so signally Peloponnesian incompetence at sea,
the other Athenian helplessness on land, where the enemy could
concentrate), but which had very little effect on the course of

the war. The dramatic contrast is there, in the events and therefore in Thucydides' narrative.

Then comes the third episode of this tremendous section of
the *History*, the *stasis*, the civil war at Kerkyra, aggravated by
the war between Athens and the Peloponnese because each faction called in the help of one or the other of the combatants. We
get the vivid narrative of the fighting in the city, the brief
moment of light when Nikostratos, the Athenian commander of
a small squadron, displays not only superb skill and gallantry
in battle but singular humanity and intelligence in an attempt
to end the civil strife. Then, on the arrival of a larger fleet and
other commanders from Athens, massacre again and treachery,
and all the other evils of *stasis*. Then at last Thucydides cannot
refrain from comment. It is not that he praises or condemns
either side in the struggle, or the conduct of any individual.
Nikostratos gets no praise, the other Athenians no blame; he
still confines himself to relating what happened. But he comments on civil strife, as it affected Kerkyra first and spread
thence to other cities during the war: its extreme violence, the
endless revenge (for each act of revenge was justified as the
righting of a wrong), the unthinking party spirit which made
men regard every moderate, every person who wanted to prevent violence and treachery, as a traitor to his own side; above
all, the unceasing suspicion which made negotiation almost impossible, and caused such agreements as were entered into to be
broken at the earliest opportunity. What could end that except,
as at Kerkyra, for a time, the virtual extinction of one party?
It is this which compels Thucydides to pause and comment, in
language as concentrated as his thought, language which one
feels he himself was forging to express what had not been expressed before, thoughts which stirred him to the depths, and
are indeed very different from anything that had occurred to
Herodotos, who accepted life as he saw it. Toward the end of
this account of the results of *stasis* Thucydides writes: οὕτω πᾶσα
ἰδέα κατέστη κακοτροπίας διὰ τὰς στάσεις τῷ Ἑλληνικῷ, καὶ τὸ εὔηθες,
οὗ τὸ γενναῖον πλεῖστον μετέχει, καταγελασθὲν ἠφανίσθη (iii 83.1):

"In this way every kind of wickedness took root in the Greek world, and that simplicity of character in which nobility has the largest part was laughed out of court and disappeared. Society was divided into two camps, and no trust was possible between them; for no word was strong enough, no oath awful enough, to end the quarrel, but all, if for a moment one party got the upper hand, calculating how hopeless was the quest for security, simply took steps in self-defense and were quite incapable of trusting anyone." Yet there are those who have read Thucydides, presumably, and can say that he was a child of his age, a pupil of the *Sophistai* and indifferent to the moral issue, or a determinist, as others have said of Herodotos, for whom the moral issue does not exist.

The section of the *History* that covers the first ten years of the war, the Archidamian War, to the peace of Nikias, that is, books ii, iii, iv, and the first twenty-four chapters of book v, can be divided, though not formally, into three parts. (I would stress this, that it is not a formal division; Thucydides is not dividing by artifice, or for any artistic reason.) The first part, which is book ii, covering the first three years, illustrates the general strategic structure, so to speak, of the war, the war of a sea power against a land power. Except for the *epitaphios*, a very great exception, for this shows, in part, what the war was about: "this was Athens, whose fate, *and whose conduct*, and so her ἦθος, was to be so vitally affected by the war"—except for this speech the rest relates a series of military events or quasi-military, like the pestilence, some of them quite indecisive, others decisive in themselves but contributing very little to the issue of the struggle, except in this one particular: Athens was declared to be morally the aggressor, because of her rule, often arbitrary rule, over other Greek states, and Sparta and her allies were the liberators. Thucydides says that at the beginning most of the Greek world was enthusiastic for Sparta; but the Spartans and their allies were technically the aggressors because it was they who declared war and would not listen to Athenian proposals for arbitration. And it was they who must *win* the war; a stalemate was a victory for Athens, whose empire would be left intact. But it would not be a very inspiring victory, especially to the adventurous Athenians, and they were not satisfied. The second part of Thucydides' account of the ten years' war covers the next two years, and contains, besides some vivid narratives of action (the escape of half the garrison from Plataia as well as the fighting at Kerkyra), those impressive chapters on Mytilene, Plataia, and on civil war, on which a word has already been said. The third part, from c. 84 of book iii to c. 24 of book v, recounts unexpected and nearly decisive victories, first of Athens, then of Sparta, when the former succeeds in both damaging Spartan prestige and doing her harm by land, and, later, Sparta, by the genius and daring of Brasidas, discovers a way of attacking the maritime empire of Athens; since each side experiences almost unhoped-for success and wholly unexpected defeat, both are ready to make peace after ten years of fighting. It will be worth while, I think, to see in what manner Thucydides, "even he, the scientific historian, though even he gives way occasionally to his sense of dramatic effect," deals with some events of this period. We have, of course, no time to do more than get a glimpse of him which I suppose is for that very reason misleading; the glimpse will be of his method of narrating successive events. We must bear in mind that he was always conscious of the need for an accurate chronology.

Let us take, to begin with, the first thirty-three chapters of book ii. (C. 34 begins the Funeral Speech. Why do classical scholars continue to call what are really *paragraphs* in a Greek or Latin author "chapters"? In an English context the word is most misleading. Thucydides' "chapters" are paragraphs, some very long, but paragraphs for all that.) We have first a statement that the war proper begins with the Theban attack on Plataia,[4] then a very careful dating, not only of the time of year of this attack, but also of the war in relation to past (and so also

----

[4] There is some difficulty here, because later Thucydides seems to take the crossing of the Attic frontier by the Peloponnesians as the true beginning of the war. I have dealt with this in my *Commentary*, Vol. II.

to future) events. Then, for four chapters, the attack and its failure; after that, the final preparations for war on both sides, meetings with allies, and other such matters; a list of the allies, very meager by the way; then cc. 10, 11, 12, final moves of the Peloponnesians and their allies the Boeotians to the frontier of Attica, with a last-minute attempt to get Athens to give way— "this day," says the Spartan messenger, "will be the beginning of great evils for Greece,"—and in c. 13 an account in some detail of the military and financial resources of Athens given to his countrymen by Perikles, whose influence was supreme. This last serves also as a reminder, both to Perikles' hearers and to Thucydides' readers, of the strategy, the almost inevitable strategy, to be adopted by both sides: Athens cannot defend her land, her troops being outnumbered three to one, but she can retire behind her walls. By the ordinary soldier's view of things the ravaging of her land should be enough to bring her to terms; a city cannot afford to lose all its harvest. But Athens could; she was already used to importing a good part of her food and also timber for her ships, and she was financially strong enough to import more for a long time to come. Also, by the ordinary methods of warfare, a walled city, resolutely defended, was impregnable except to hunger, but Athens could not be reduced by hunger, for her walls ran down to the sea and enclosed the harbor within them. They were long, but she had enough troops to man them, and their length meant also that they enclosed a space large enough, or nearly so, for the whole population to withdraw into. All this Thucydides does not explain in so many words, doubtless because it was all familiar to his readers, but mainly because here, as elsewhere, he lets his narrative of *events* tell its own story; so what he does here is to give the figures (or some of them; we must not overpraise him), financial and military statistics. Perikles' advice, then, agreed to by the people in principle some time back, was now adopted, and everyone from the countryside came within the walls, bringing what furniture they could with them, leaving behind as little as possible for the enemy: with heavy hearts, for, more

than most Greeks, they had lived in the country, coming into
the town only for festivals or for necessary trade or for some
great political occasion, and they now, says Thucydides, felt as
they would if they were leaving each his own city—that is, of
course, as we should say, his own *country*. And they began to
grumble as they crowded into Athens and settled down where
they could. By early summer the large Peloponnesian force
arrived, crossed the border, and began to ravage the land, and
when the Athenians saw with their own eyes from within the
city their farms burning, they gathered in groups and their
anger grew till it burst into loud demands that they be led out
to fight the enemy and drive him away, and Perikles was upbraided for cowardice. He remained in control, however, and
only the cavalry made sorties from the walls to intercept enemy
raiding parties that came too near.

The Peloponnesians retired after a month or a little more to
see to their own harvests, and also because supplies in the field
would not hold out much longer. (The war was like our modern
wars in this, that the whole populations of cities were involved,
or might be, and therefore their whole economy affected; they
were not wars waged by small professional armies, with the
main body of citizens concerned only with paying for them and
patriotic applause.) The Athenians had already sent out a fleet
round the Peloponnese to see what damage they could do by
raiding; they land here and there, are foiled in one place by
Brasidas, and sail on to strengthen their alliances in the west.
Another Athenian squadron went north to Lokris. The inhabitants of Aigina were ejected as being in dangerous proximity
to Peiraeus. There was an eclipse of the sun. (*We* can add here:
on August 5, about 5:22 in the afternoon.) Athens made an
alliance with a powerful Thracian king because of her difficulties up north in Chalkidike and Macedonia. The fleet operating
in the west captured two places from Corinth or Corinthian
sympathizers and won over Kephallenia, and returned home.
The squadron in Lokrian waters takes a small island and forti-
fies it. In the autumn the Athenians invaded the Megarid and

did there what the Peloponnesians had done to Attica earlier. The Corinthians, during the winter, recover one of the two places captured by the Athenians in the west but fail to win back Kephallenia. (With the Peloponnesians away, the Athenians can move out by land for a short time; with the Athenian fleet returned home, the Corinthians could move out, for a little, by sea.) Then in the same winter, toward the end of the year, which for Thucydides is from one spring equinox to the next, or a little earlier than that,[5] the Athenians held their solemn ceremony celebrated every year in wartime for those who had fallen during the year, and Perikles delivered the *epitaphios*, the funeral speech, which, Thucydides tells us, on this occasion, the first of many others, perhaps, in what might prove to be a long war, Perikles turned into a reminder to his fellow citizens, not only of the courage of the dead, but of what sort of city they had died for; what was this Athens of theirs, with its temples bright and shining, only recently rebuilt after the Persian destruction, the great gateway of the Acropolis not quite finished even, the work on it being interrupted by the war? What was this Athens, with its enviable laws, its beloved freedom and variety, its many festivals?

Here surely we have an instance of what Aristotle meant in saying that a historian can only record, and record all of the relevant events within a period, in the order of their happening. In this case, as well, almost all of them insignificant events, and even the most important of them, the invasion of Attica, of little account for the issue of the war and of no special military interest. But reflect on what Thucydides in fact achieves by letting the story speak for itself. First, a picture of what a war between a power on land and another supreme at sea will be like—a series of pinpricks, unless one side or the other can find out how to deliver a more decisive blow; and with that, an Athenian victory, as Perikles foresaw, for the purpose of the war was the overthrow of Athenian dominion. It was all going according to his plans, which have been explained in book i,

---

[5] I discuss this problem in an appendix in the second volume of my *Commentary*.

before war broke out. Victory was assured if the Athenians held out, but this was a big "if"; would they hold out, year after year, watching the hated enemy lay waste their land? That demanded leadership both strong and consistent, and great self-control in the general body of the citizens who could at any time listen to another demagogue and turn Perikles out; they were known for their enterprise and adventurous spirit, for their optimism and fickleness. That danger is clearly indicated. Besides that, an apparently very small thing—Brasidas is mentioned. He foils a small Athenian enterprise as he was, later, to foil the major Athenian plans, and a little emphasis is given by Thucydides to this in itself trivial happening: Brasidas was the first Spartan in this war to receive the thanks of his city.

Thus by a simple statement of what happened, Thucydides does just what is required of him both as artist and historian, namely, prepare us for the narrative to come. He even does something to prepare us for the unforeseeable, the sudden outbreak of the pestilence when that sunny and confident, yet self-controlled city that Perikles has so eloquently described was changed at once into a crowd of sick people, so many so quickly dead that all could not be buried immediately, and a crowd not only sick but demoralized. Unforeseeable, says Perikles, and indeed Greece had not been a country liable to pestilence, though there had been sporadic outbreaks of this same disease elsewhere, of no great violence, shortly before. Perikles was known for his foresight, πρόνοια, and prided himself on it, but no one could foresee a thing of this kind. That is all it is in Thucydides, an unforeseeable event, not, as it might have been in Herodotos, the sort of event that would happen, οἷον ἂν γένοιτο, to a people hitherto so prosperous and successful. But the extent of the disaster (more than a quarter of the whole population died and many of the survivors were crippled or their health seriously impaired), not its occurrence but its extent, was directly due to the war, to the policy of bringing all the people within the walls, crowded and living in unhealthy conditions; a normally healthy people soon succumbed to a new disease. For that too Thucydides has prepared us, telling us how they had all crowded in and how few had proper dwellings. It is, of course, quite a simple matter, this narrative; I do not want to suggest that Thucydides displays in this section some marvelous power denied to others; I am only trying to show how artist and historian, scientific historian, meet.

My next instances illustrate a different facet. The Peloponnesians and their allies, using their superiority on land, decide to attack Plataia, which Athens cannot succor any better than she could her own lands. After some attempts, with primitive weapons, to carry it by storm, which they had hoped to do because they so greatly outnumbered the defenders, they decided to reduce the city by hunger. They therefore built a new wall for themselves all around the city. (This served both as a shelter for the troops in rough weather and as a protection against sorties from the town or surprise attacks from without; by the same principle by which a small garrison could defend a walled town, a besieging army, with a protective wall of its own, need not be a large one. Its only duty at Plataia, for example, was to prevent food getting in or the garrison getting out; so once this wall was built, most of the Spartan forces went thankfully home. This principle Thucydides takes for granted as known to his readers.) The building of this wall is what Thucydides relates in its chronological place, the third year of the war, with a statement of the exact numbers of the besieged, 400 Plataians, 80 Athenians, and 110 women to look after them; all the rest had been evacuated to Athens (ii 78). Eighteen months or so later, on a dark and stormy night, half of that garrison escape. The story is told in a most graphic way; it is preceded by a detailed description of the Peloponnesian surrounding wall (iii 21). The description is given now, not before, when we were told simply that the wall was built, because it is now relevant; most careful and detailed plans must be made by the escaping party, and the shape and size of the chief obstacle have to be considered; it is what the Plataians must have had uppermost in their minds in making their attempt.

This is a very simple instance of a logical order of relation; here is a more subtle one. In 429 the Peloponnesians met with a defeat, a humiliating defeat at sea off Naupaktos by a small Athenian squadron, brilliantly led by Phormion with individual Athenian ships as well acting on their own initiative with great dash and enterprise, so well were they trained. (It is difficult, by the way, to picture to oneself quick maneuvering, sudden changes of speed or direction in a ship that is *rowed* by a crew of one hundred and seventy, free men too, the half of them turbulent citizens of Athens; Perikles, so the story went, when about to lead an expeditionary force, would say to himself: "Be careful; remember these are free men you are commanding, Greeks, citizens of Athens." Yet on an Athenian trireme, as Thucydides does not fail here to remind us, discipline, good order, and, in action, silence prevailed [ii 89.9]; we are always taught that these were Spartan virtues, and so they were.) After this defeat, the Peloponnesian commanders, with unwonted resilience (but Brasidas was one of them), decide to make a sudden attack by sea on the Peiraeus, at the beginning of winter and by night, the last thing that the Athenians, anyhow crowing over their recent victories, would be expecting (ii 93–94). For this the crews must carry their oars and one or two other pieces of equipment across the isthmus from west to east, and man some Megarian ships lying in harbor on the east coast. They set sail on their daring enterprise, but their hearts fail them; "it is not worth the risk." (That will be the other commander, Knemos.) Besides, it is said that the wind was against them; they do not go for the Peiraeus, but land on the island of Salamis and ravage and burn it. That caused excitement and alarm enough in Athens, and when they saw the signals, those in the city itself thought that the enemy must be in the Peiraeus, and those in the Peiraeus thought that Salamis was captured and that the Peloponnesians would be attacking them at any minute, which, says Thucydides, they could easily have done had they had enough resolution, and no wind would have stopped them. As it was, the Athenians, in considerable

confusion, rushed to man their ships, setting sail about day-
break, and the Peloponnesians retired hastily with their loot.
They were frightened as well because their ships leaked, so long
had they been laid up; they had not been put to sea since before
the war, that is, for four years at least. Observe how in this episode some details are told in the order in which they impinged
on the actors themselves; a later historian might have *begun*
his narrative with words like these: "The Peloponnesian crews
had to man ships which were not in good condition, but they
were the only ones on the eastern shore, and they had a wind
to contend with." Thucydides mentions the wind when the
Peloponnesians first decided that after all they will not go as
far as the Peiraeus, or want an excuse for not going, and the
leaky ships not till the end, for it was then that the rowers, and
still more the landlubberly soldiers on board, would begin to
get anxious.

My last example of this kind of writing is yet more complex
and more interesting; it is the story of Brasidas' march to Chalkidike in 424, early in August, and his capture of Amphipolis in
the following November or December, that decisive victory
over Athenian forces when Thucydides himself was one of the
two commanders in the field against him. During that campaign
the Athenians waged another, their ambitious invasion of Boeotia which ended in a second big victory for the enemy at the
battle of Delion, these defeats coming very soon after their own
victories of the preceding summer and the year before at Pylos,
which had made them feel capable of anything and sure of success. Thucydides' narrative of these two campaigns, by what
the great Wilamowitz called his unfortunate chronological
method (which had also been criticized by lesser men, including
Dionysios of Halikarnassos), jumps from one to the other
several times, alternating between them. In this he has not been
followed by modern historians, even though they can add but
little to what he says; they prefer Ephoros, and carefully and
tidily they relate first the one campaign and then the other. One
of these is Professor Adcock in the *Cambridge Ancient History*,

and I will draw your attention to one sentence in his summary, after he has related the events. He is discussing that ever-interesting problem, the degree of Thucydides' own responsibility for the loss of Amphipolis, and he ends thus, excusing Thucydides: "The historian had failed to be wiser than his colleagues or his countrymen who might have crushed Brasidas with half the force that was defeated at Delium."

This is how Thucydides tells the story; I will give it by the chapters, that is, paragraphs, of book iv. Cc. 66–69, in the summer of 424 the Athenians make a special effort to capture Megara and start successfully by taking the port of Nisaia from a Peloponnesian garrison which was guarding it primarily to secure political stability in Megara, where there was a strong pro-Athenian party. (The unfortunate Megarians would, all of them, have liked to be neutral, but their state lay right in the path between the two combatants.) Cc. 70–74, Brasidas was just at that moment near Corinth, making preparations for an expedition to Thrace (this is the first mention of it); he hurried toward Megara with a considerable force, and succeeded, after much maneuvering, in securing the city for the Peloponnese, though Athens retained Nisaia. Brasidas himself returned to Corinth to continue his preparations for the Thracian expedition. C. 75 is a minor campaign elsewhere. In cc. 76–77 we hear of ambitious Athenian plans to intervene in the same summer in Boeotia, not by open warfare but, it was hoped, by encouraging democratic partisans to make trouble and by having Athenian forces threaten to invade at three separate points, to paralyze activity and ultimately win the country to their side. Cc. 78–79, *at the same time*, Brasidas marches to Trachis (through allied country, thus far) and thence, by a combination of daring, trickery, and cajolery, through Thessaly to Macedonia, where he is welcomed by king Perdikkas, now an ally of Sparta, and by the Chalkidians; and at the mention of the latter we remember, if we are wise, a short paragraph (iv 7) inserted in its proper chronological place in the midst of the story of the Pylos campaign of the previous year. This paragraph relates an incident in Chalkidike, utterly unimportant in itself but one that reminds us that the Athenian position in that area, nominally within the Athenian empire, is still weak and the Chalkidians still hostile. Cc. 80–81 give the motive of this expedition under Brasidas and the reason why Sparta was ready to sponsor it and let Brasidas go; we go backward, that is, in time, and then forward into the future when the effect of Brasidas' general honesty and moderation of character is related. Cc. 82–88, the Athenians declare war on Perdikkas and take precautions in Thrace. Brasidas has difficulties with Perdikkas, then marches across Chalkidike shortly before the grape harvest and wins over Akanthos and later Stagiros; and Thucydides takes the opportunity of reporting a speech by Brasidas and thus of stressing the nature and importance of the campaign, and in some measure showing the secret of his success; incidentally also how light the Athenian rule was, the democratic ways of the Greek city, and the lack of enthusiasm for the liberator.

Cc. 89–101, the campaign near Delion in Boeotia; the Athenian plans go astray; they are forced to fight a pitched battle and are completely defeated. The story is given in detail. At the end, in four lines, the death of Sitalkes, the most powerful of the Thracian kings and ally of Athens. Cc. 102–109, in the same winter, Brasidas by a sudden and rapid march reaches Amphipolis on the river Strymon, which had been settled by Athens thirteen years before, after more than one unsuccessful attempt; his unexpected appearance and the moderation of his proposals overawed the inhabitants, who admitted him. Thucydides with a small squadron of seven ships nearly a day's sail away just managed to save Eion, the port at the mouth of the river. A note is here added on the strategic and political importance of Amphipolis to Athens, the danger of Brasidas' marching further into the empire, and the impact on Athenian feeling of these two unexpected defeats. All the advantages won by the victories of 425 and 424 were lost.

Do you see what Thucydides has done? We hear of Brasidas' doings in the same way as the Athenians themselves did. This, remember, was the moment of their greatest success, and so of their greatest optimism: "everything must go right; they expected nothing to oppose them (ἠξίουν σφίσι μηδὲν ἐναντιοῦσθαι": iv 65.4). Brasidas at Corinth and everything not going so well at Megara? A nuisance: ἐναντίωμά τι (69.1), *un petit dérangement*, but no matter; we have grander schemes in Boeotia. Brasidas at Trachis with a small but select force on his way to Thrace? Oh, our Thessalian friends will surely prevent him going further. "Have you heard the news? Brasidas is in Macedonia." "Is he, by Zeus? We will warn our men up there to be on their guard, but we must not allow it to interfere with our Boeotian plans." They did not, and disaster followed. Then, at the end, the importance of Amphipolis, when the Athenians realize what they have lost. That is how Thucydides lets the events tell their own tale; no need for a summary to explain things, certainly not in self-excuse, or to say that half the army that fought at Delion would have been enough to crush Brasidas; just tell the facts in their due order. Thucydides could not be more accurate, more scientific, if he had had the Gregorian calendar and a modern chronometer, and instead of "shortly before the grape harvest" had written "August 15, 2.25 P.M., Greenwich time, and do not forget that that is 1 hr. 35 min. behind Athens and Akanthos." But it is also perfect art, where he appears to do no more than just tell the facts in their proper order. It is simply that he has done the work first, including, what must have been difficult, getting a fairly full account of the battle of Delion, fought when he himself was in Thrace; if he has done that work well, then he was in a position to relate the events, in the most direct way possible. The reader draws his own conclusions, as he does when the Spartan trial of the Plataian prisoners follows the Athenian debate about Mytilene, and the great expedition to Sicily the comparatively unimportant one to Melos.

Similarly in some of the speeches, for example, the Mytilenean at Olympia, when they relate, from their point of view, something of the history of the Athenian management of the empire; we are now going back to the past, but this is the occasion when this past, or rather the Mytilenean version of it, is in the minds of the speakers and must be brought to the minds not only of their hearers but of Thucydides' readers. It is the logical place for it in the *History*. This seems natural enough in speeches, and we hardly notice it, but the same principle is often at work in the narrative of events.

Another conclusion may be drawn, in passing, from this analysis of one part of Thucydides' work. I cannot follow Collingwood (*Idea of History*, pp. 29–31) in his belief that Thucydides was not, like Herodotos, interested in facts, but, like Plato, in general laws, and so was unhistorical, as Plato was. In his *History* (which is all we have of him) Thucydides is more recorder than philosopher, even though we may feel certain that he was always thinking of general laws—but thinking about them rather than formulating them and giving them to the world.

VII

Thucydides (*Continued*)

IN THE LAST LECTURE I was describing Thucydides' way of letting the story tell itself, with as little comment of his own as possible. There is, of course, some comment, as about the effect on Athenian war policy of Perikles' death or the bearing of Brasidas' personal character on the feelings of Athenian subject allies. This has been often observed, sometimes well observed as by Cornford, whose book *Thucydides Mythistoricus* includes so much that is good in a perversely misshapen setting, and by Thibaudet, *La Campagne avec Thucydide*, written, as it were, in the trenches of the 1914–1918 war, when the terrible reality of Thucydides' *History* was once more felt and learned. I shall have occasion later to quarrel with one opinion of Thibaudet's on an important matter; for the moment I will only say that it is a book to be read, as it is short and contains a great deal of sense. "L'histoire," he says (p. 49), "telle que la propose Thucydide, unit et fait servir l'un à l'autre deux caractères qui, semble-t-il, s'excluent: la plus grande exactitude matérielle et la plus grande généralité. D'ailleurs, quand on croit qu'elles s'excluent, c'est qu'on ne pense pas à l'art, qui les implique au contraire toutes deux et emploie l'une à la perfection de l'autre." ("History, as Thucydides gives it to us, unites two characteristics which it might seem are mutually exclusive, and makes the one serve the other: the greatest exactness in its facts and the widest generality. Further, when we believe that these are mutually exclusive, it is because we are forgetting art, which in truth implies both and uses, rigorously, the one for the perfection of the other.") And again: "La dernière chose d'ailleurs à laquelle il pensait était bien . . . la beauté. Mais elle résultait nécessairement de sa double recherche du vrai et du type." That is, in good history, as well as in poetry (though in a different fashion), the general is embodied in particular instances, and Aristotle, though so sensible in distinguishing the two, was wrong in the special distinction he makes. And in good history there is, inevitably, both science and art, and modern scholars are quite wrong in saying, or implying, that one is, practically speaking, incompatible with the other. The historian, in his narrative, cannot help being an artist, a good, or alas so often, a bad one. The scholar may content himself with collecting and presenting the evidence (as Winston Churchill says he is doing), which is invaluable; but if he goes further and narrates, he must do his best as an artist if he is to be a good historian—not just as if he lived in "antiquity," as though all ancient historians from Herodotos to Ammianus Marcellinus wrote alike, and modern historians were happily free from the laws which govern the artist's work. They often think they are free, and that is when they try to do two things at once, collect and sift and examine the evidence and also narrate, and suppose that they are being scientific and learned if they do this necessary first part of the work not first, but simultaneously, by putting it in footnotes, or even subsequently, by putting what should be read first into appendices. Thucydides, not because he was an "ancient" writer, but because he was a sensible man and clearheaded, did his work in the right order, and then presented the finished work to the public, as the architect presents the building, not only without the many first sketches and plans, but without the scaffolding.[1]

When we say that Thucydides lets the facts as he narrates them tell their own story, we mean that we can see, if we read intelligently, the generality that is there for ourselves, as we can see the poet's. But in Thucydides maybe we should, just in this connection, make special inquiry about the many speeches in the *History*, because there, men say, not in the narrative, is

---

[1] I take the metaphor from Cornford. It is a good one; many a scholar seems to prefer a history disguised by its scaffolding, as though it were best not to see clearly what the writer intended.

the generality to be found. Did Thucydides write the speeches, whether, as many have thought, entirely out of his own head, or on a basis of what had been said? I will only say that, for myself, I think first that he always did his best to get information about the arguments and the manner of the speeches, and secondly that there must have been wide differences between the material he could collect for one speech and that for another. To take two extremes: we have other evidence that the arguments found in the first speech of Perikles at the end of book i, when he is urging the Athenians to stand firm and reject the ultimatum presented by the Peloponnesians, were in fact arguments used at that time, and we may be sure that Perikles, on more than one occasion, formulated them; Thucydides, as likely as not, heard the speech himself; on the other hand, for the speeches of the Plataians and Thebans after the surrender of Plataia it is very difficult to see how he got any evidence. Even if for that particular speech of Perikles Thucydides did not happen to be in Athens to hear it and got only a brief report on it, "Perikles led the way in the case against accepting the ultimatum, using the well-known arguments," and, for the other two, there was someone to tell him "the Plataians made a most moving speech—the usual thing, of course, their conduct in the Persian Wars, the oaths taken by all the Greek states to respect their territory—but very well done," and "the Theban speech was full of envy and hatred," even so, he would have been in a position to construct a historically more accurate speech for the former than for the latter, because he knew Perikles' politics, must have heard him speak, and knew well the arguments he was accustomed to put forward. We can in consequence see a real and an important difference between the speeches. The Plataian is more like "the kind of speech that men in the position of the Plataians at that time and with their past record, might have made," that is, οἷον ἂν γένοιτο, poetic in Aristotle's sense of the phrase, and Perikles' speech is more like "the speeches which he in fact delivered more than once in that crisis," at least οἷον ἐγένετο, though not precisely ὅπερ ἐγένετο. (Thucydides of course, introduces the speeches with τοιάδε ἔλεξεν, unlike Herodotos in this, who does appear to give "the very words," as the poet does.) Important, however, as this distinction is, it is not so decisive as some have thought, for even if Thucydides had possessed among his notes verbatim reports of every speech he gives, and of a hundred others, the selection and the presentation is his, just as he had verbatim reports of at least some public documents and gives them thus, and others in his own words, and these sometimes in detail (as iv 16; see also p. 118, n.), sometimes in briefest outline. This selection and presentation is purely subjective—subject, that is, to the historian's own judgment,—and in selecting and presenting he is obeying the laws that govern the writing of history and at the same time those that govern art; and his work may be well or ill done, both as historian and as artist, for in his case the two coincide. Grote had genuine documents enough in that part of his history that deals with the wars of Philip of Macedon: several speeches of Demosthenes, some by his opponents; he refers to them, translates some passages in full, others in summary, and all this selection and presentation is his own, entirely subjective. The words of the translation or summary are his own; hence too this whole narrative has that unity of style which we especially ascribe to the ancients. It can be, and has been said, that his narrative, which includes these extracts from Demosthenes, be it ever so accurate in the scholarly sense, is colored by the prejudices and preconceptions of a nineteenth-century English liberal. Of course it is; all human work is subject to limitations of time and place; how could it be otherwise? All that we are entitled to ask of the historian is that he be intelligent, that is, that he be not a ninny about his own age and its predilections, that he work hard to find all the evidence there is, and that he have a regard for the truth. Only, that cannot but be, in the end, the truth as he sees it. We also ask that he be able to write.

With this somewhat long digression safely passed we may return to our main theme, which is this: many have noted the dramatic contrasts in Thucydides, especially that between the attack on Melos and the expedition to Syracuse, with the implied but seldom expressed opinion that in some way the course of events was not as Thucydides says it was; that he has doctored the true picture quite unintentionally, unconsciously, because his preconceptions were such that he saw things wrong. According to the best known and the best argued of these views, Cornford's, he saw things as an Aeschylean tragedy, with the Athenians in the story of the Syracusan expedition individualized in their leader Alkibiades, led on by *Apate*, a sort of spirit of deceit—led on to their crimes and so to their doom. Cornford can even find something "dramatic," i.e., not strictly historical, in the fact that Thucydides does not tell us, though Plutarch does, that it was Alkibiades who moved the decree that the citizens of Melos should be massacred or enslaved: "he is being reserved for a more dramatic appearance, to speak in favour of the expedition to Syracuse" (p. 186); yet, assuming that Plutarch is right, Thucydides might have put in at least a quiet Ἀλκιβιάδου γνώμη, as he does in relating the similar decree against Skione moved by Kleon (as noted by Cornford, p. 124, n. 1), who is also, it is said, "reserved" for the great event, his failure at Amphipolis. But there are other such conjunctions, just as impressive but with no such Aeschylean moral, such as the two I mentioned in the preceding chapter, the Funeral Speech and the narrative of the pestilence, and the Mytilenean campaign followed by the fall of Plataia. All agree, whether they suppose these stories to be doctored or not by the unconscious need for dramatic effect, that the way the contrast is brought out is by the use of speeches. Without the "dialogue" the Melian affair would sink to the level of its inherent military unimportance; without the speeches the defeat of Mytilene and the surrender of Plataia would be minor events in the war. Or rather, without them Thucydides would have had, in the modern manner, to have written pages of explanation of what he thought was their significance; with the speeches he can let the events explain themselves in the artist's manner. But already we see that in one of these cases only one half is a speech, the *epitaphios*; the other, equally impressive, is a direct account of what happened in the pestilence, written in what Cornford (pp. 54–56) regarded as Thucydides' earlier manner as truthful recorder of events before he was overtaken, or taken in hand, by his dramatic spirit. This narrative of the pestilence is, in fact, the one which illustrates best the union of the particular and the general, of which Thibaudet speaks, and of science and art in Thucydides (if "union" is the right word to apply to two aspects of the same thing); we have the detailed narrative of the symptoms ("so that they may be recognized if the disease returns")—what could be more scientific? Careful observation, with the intention of widening the bounds of knowledge; the physical suffering and the dejection of spirits; the ineffectual attempts to deal with it (the doctors had had no previous knowledge of it, and they and others most attentive to the sick all caught it the quicker); the demoralization which followed when there were not enough left to look after the sufferers or even bury the dead—all described in Thucydides' individual and graphic way. Nobody has yet suggested that the pestilence did not occur just then, and take the form and have the results which he describes; yet the "dramatic" effect, coming as this narrative does immediately after the Funeral Speech, is overwhelming.

Another, equally eloquent, contrast is to be found in the description of Athenian conduct in the civil war in Kerkyra in 427 (iii 70–85); I referred briefly to it in the preceding chapter, but it is worth retelling in some detail too for its own sake.

Kerkyra had had a defensive alliance with Athens since before the war began and Athens had saved her from falling again under the domination of Corinth, her mother city; she had till now, in the first four years of the war (431–427), avoided nearly all active fighting. The civil war began in this way: Corinth had had for several years a number of prisoners of war from Kerkyra; she now released them on the understanding that as soon as they got home they would bring Kerkyra into the

Peloponnesian alliance. They were, in the main, the wealthier people who wanted this; they started up their activities by laying an accusation against the democratic leader of being an agent of a foreign aggressive power with the design of bringing the city into subjection to Athens. He was acquitted on this charge, and at once brought a countercharge of sacrilege against five prominent persons among his enemies. They were charged with having, over a long period, cut stakes from a vineyard belonging to a temple (which, presumably, they were renting); the fine due was enormous. (The charge was more or less like one of illegal currency transactions in revolutionary states at the present day.) All compromise being refused, the oligarchs retorted by open violence; some of them burst into the council chamber and killed the democratic leaders. Fighting then broke out generally, with varying fortunes at first. The slaves, who were numerous in Kerkyra, were invited by both sides to help, with promises of freedom. The oligarchs, to prevent an attack by their foes on the central and wealthiest part of the city, burned it down. Next day a small Athenian squadron of twelve ships, with some infantry on board, arrived; they included the two special courier ships, manned by Athenian citizens only.

These vessels were under the command of Nikostratos, who at once tried to put an end to the fighting by persuading the two parties to accept a compromise and to live at peace with each other, with the city in full alliance with Athens and bringing to trial only the ten most guilty of starting the civil war. These ten had in fact already left the city, and they were condemned *in absentia*. Nikostratos was then about to depart (he had Naupaktos, an important Athenian post, two days' sail away, to defend) when the Kerkyra democrats, now of course in control of the town, begged him to leave five of his own ships behind as a guarantee of the settlement, and take five of their own instead. He agreed, and they at once drafted their political enemies to man them—an old trick, used, for example, by Polykrates of Samos (above, p. 89), though understandable enough in these conditions. The oligarchs, however, fearful of being taken away to Athens as prisoners, refused to go on board, and, declining to listen to Nikostratos' assurances, took refuge as suppliants in a temple. Thereupon the democrats, crying out that it was obvious that their enemies were already plotting to destroy the recent agreement and overthrow the constitution, denounced them and would have started slaughtering any of their enemies they could get at then and there if Nikostratos had not prevented them. Finally four hundred of these suppliant oligarchs were removed to a small island off the coast.

Four or five days later a Peloponnesian fleet of fifty-three vessels, which had been getting ready for sea for some time, arrived off the city and prepared to attack. The men of Kerkyra, in a panic, hurriedly manned their sixty ships and put to sea as each ship was got ready, though the Athenians urged them to allow *them* to hold off the enemy till their ships were all ready and could sail out together and in good order. As they approached the enemy fleet in this straggling fashion, two ships at once deserted, in others fighting broke out among the crews, and there was no longer any pretense of order. The Peloponnesians were thus enabled to leave only twenty out of their fifty-three to deal with the Kerkyraioi, while with the rest they faced the Athenian twelve; these latter, outnumbered, had to exercise great care; they attacked one wing, sinking an enemy vessel.[2] The Peloponnesians nervously formed themselves into a circle, and the Athenians sailed round and round them endeavoring to throw them into confusion (by threats of attack on single ships, making them retreat into an ever-diminishing circle in which their oars were likely to become entangled—just what had led to the brilliant victory two years before). The other Peloponnesian squadron, seeing what was happening, now joined the rest, ignoring the Kerkyraioi; and together the fifty bore down upon the Athenians, who retired slowly, backing water, that is, with their prows still facing the enemy and thus

[2] There is the well-known story of Foch in the 1914–1918 war: "My center is crushed, my left wing is in retreat, my right hard-pressed; *j'attaque.*" But Thucydides did not need the fine rhetoric.

ready to attack any Peloponnesian ship that might advance more boldly than the rest: a particularly brave thing, this, and requiring steady nerve and great confidence in their officers, for in ships that were rowed the crews still had their backs to the enemy. Meantime they called to the Kerkyraioi to get back to the harbor as best they might "while *we* retreat at our leisure and the enemy are all in line against *us*."

Nothing could be better, could it, than the conduct of Nikostratos and his Athenians? these imperialists, who take control when their allies are hopeless, who show themselves politically humane and intelligent, in battle courageous and skillful beyond any normal skill and courage. It was just as their envious enemies the Corinthians had described them when trying, before the outbreak of war, to waken the torpid Spartans to an understanding of their danger; and just as Perikles had hoped that they would show themselves, a whole people of aristocrats, free but disciplined, generous, daring, and daring because dangers were intelligently understood; "at least none of our subjects can complain that we are not worthy to rule." Well, three days later, another and larger Athenian fleet arrived, of sixty vessels, under the command of Eurymedon; the Peloponnesians, who had not made use of their temporary superiority, scuttled away home as fast as possible, with Nikostratos and his squadron following them, it seems, to defend Naupaktos. The Athenians and the pro-Athenian democrats of Kerkyra were now in complete and secure control, and the latter took full advantage of it to get the better of their enemies. They attacked them in the streets, or put them on trial and condemned all to death. "For seven days while Eurymedon and his sixty ships were with them" the massacre continued; against some the charge of attempting to overthrow the constitution was brought, against others personal enmities were indulged, or debtors would seize the opportunity of getting rid of their creditors. Every kind of murder took place, and when Eurymedon sailed away, the four hundred survivors of the oligarchs who had escaped to the mainland seized some strong points and raided the island from these, causing great distress.

The dramatic contrast is there, between Nikostratos and his men on one side and on the other the ordinary Athenians, who do not often behave as imperialists should; but it is all to be found in direct and vivid narrative. There is no word of praise for Nikostratos or blame of Eurymedon; we do not, for all that, doubt what Thucydides thought of them, nor has anyone questioned the truth of the narrative.

As an appendix Thucydides tells us how this same Eurymedon two years later, on his way to Sicily with another fleet, put into Kerkyra to relieve the town of the depredations of the marauding oligarchs who, with the help of mercenaries, had now seized a strong point on the island itself, having desperately burned their boats (iv 46–48). Eurymedon defeats them and they surrender, expressly to Athens and not to their political enemies in Kerkyra, but the latter by a trick persuaded them to break the terms of the peace, and so they were all handed over to the democrats, who, with many a refinement of cruelty, killed them. The democrats were encouraged to this by Eurymedon and his colleague, who had made it clear that, as they had to go on to Sicily, they did not want another to have the glory of conducting the Kerkyraian oligarchs as prisoners to Athens. Thus, says Thucydides, the civil war ended, for the time, when one side had been practically exterminated.

The "dramatic" character of Thucydides' *History* is thus, fundamentally, implicit in the events: they were dramatic, and a true history, that is, a scientific history, if well written, that is, if a work of art, will reveal them so. That Thucydides, furthermore, was conscious of their dramatic character is true; that is only to say that he was an intelligent man. To say also that he was a child of his time, that he had certain preconceptions of which he was barely conscious, is as true of him as of all other men. To understand, if we can, what those preconceptions were is a task worth undertaking, but for myself I am confident that a dramatic conception of events, of a kind that would make him inevitably and unconsciously distort the true picture, was not one of them; certainly not a drama of the Aeschylean type, as Cornford thought. Other historians too, and among them the most modern, have been conscious of "dramatic" incidents, or of the dramatic irony of history, including some of those who have written histories of ancient Greece; the difference lies largely in our feeling that we must express our views, underline the drama, or point out the moral, where Herodotos and Thucydides, better artists, leave the story to speak for itself. It would, as well, be to the last degree misleading to suggest that Thucydides' *History* is arranged as a series of such dramatic contrasts; on the contrary, the run of the narrative, the structure of its various parts, differs from time to time according to the run of the events which he conscientiously records. I should be the last to give the impression, wittingly, that Thucydides had some prearranged pattern in his mind; but there is some truth in the statement that the Athenian people are the tragic heroes of the drama of the Peloponnesian Wars, as Thucydides understood it, and, therefore, as we do: heroes of a noble character—ἄνδρες χρηστοί, "good men," in Aristotle's words,—liable more than most, perhaps, to faults of character and judgment which led direct to their ruin, faults which arose, not like those of Achilles or Othello from the noble elements in their character, but from fickleness, a certain conceit of themselves, and a hardness of heart which, in them, was to be found side by side with fine intelligence, discipline, generosity, and a wonderful self-knowledge. It is interesting in this to compare Aristophanes with Thucydides; in so many ways their pictures of Athens are complementary, but in one thing at least they differ. Aristophanes, both in his earliest extant play when his Athenians were full of fight, and in *The Peace* which celebrated (as so many hoped) the end of the fighting, shows that hardness, a streak of cruelty, which was part of the Athenian, perhaps of the Greek character, whereas Thucydides was distressed by cruelty and violence more than other men. That is why so much of his story is not of militarily decisive events, but "this is what the war was like; this is how people behave in war"; people of an ordinary sort of goodness deteriorate; βίαιος διδάσκαλος ὁ πόλεμος, "war is a violent taskmaster." One is tempted to say of the Athenians of Thucydides that they

> Like the base Indian threw a pearl away,
> Richer than all his tribe;

only, not like the base Indian, for they knew what they were doing, both the value of the pearl and that by their own folly they were losing it. Nor, after all, was the pearl thrown away; Thucydides, with others, preserved it for such of us as care to look at it.

It is hardly possible to do more than glance, in the time at my disposal, at some aspects of Thucydides' political thought; and I again choose some which illustrate as well his method of narration. Herodotos, happy man, had as his theme almost the whole of known humanity and the miracle of the Greek victory: he could, so to speak, afford to be light of heart at the spectacle of human folly; Thucydides' theme was itself somber, and one, not multifarious. Hence Herodotos' digressions—his real digressions, not simply his variety,—his discursiveness, which contrasts so sharply with the strong concentration of Thucydides on his single theme—a concentration largely the effect of self-control, reflected so well in his closely knit language, not at all the result of indifference to other times and subjects. In this respect, and only in this, I think, is it proper to call Thucydides' whole method dramatic, that is, shaped like an Attic tragedy, by contrast with the epic manner of Herodotos (as Cornford, p. 138). His theme is the war which came near to destroying what had been saved by the victory over Persia. Herodotos had said that the earthquake at Delos in 490 was the portent of evils to come for Greece, partly at the hands of Persia, partly from wars for primacy among the leading states of Greece, but he did not live to see how true his prophecy was to be. Moreover, while in Herodotos history is largely the story of individuals, in Thucydides it is the history of states, or rather, of people in

communities or groups; he was interested in individual character, in Themistokles, Perikles, Nikias, Brasidas, Kleon, and
thought their influence on events important, but his theme is
the behavior of peoples, in wartime, what they do and suffer.
Athenaioi, Lakedaimonioi, Thebaioi are his principal characters,
Plataieis, Melioi, Mykalessioi, are the smaller ones who suffer,
like Polonius and Ophelia in the play. It is worth telling, this
last story, that of Mykalessos. It was a small city, in Boeotia
and so involved in the war, and not far from the sea, but lying
off the main routes of armies on the other side of the mountain
that slopes down to the Gulf of Euboea opposite to Chalkis,
high up, and never expecting the approach of an enemy; its wall
was in disrepair. Some Thracian mercenary troops, who had
arrived in Athens too late for the purpose for which they had
been recruited, were sent back again (for Athens, having spent
so much on splendid equipment for the expedition to Sicily,
could not afford to keep them unemployed) with orders to do
such damage to the enemy as they could on the way. They
landed near Mykalessos and went up the hill by night; then,
soon after dawn, broke into the unsuspecting city, killing all
whom they met, men, women, and children, even pack animals,
any living thing they saw; the worst was when they fell upon
the largest school in the place where the children had just arrived, and killed them all. When help came from Thebes, these
savages fled, fighting, down to their ships again, and on the
shore very many of them were killed, for the ships kept out of
range of arrow and javelin and the Thracians could not swim.
The disaster to Mykalessos was as great as any in the war, says
Thucydides, forced again into comment, and the most sorrow-
ful. Such cities suffer like the weak in a play, but, once more,
this does not mean that he did not record, as accurately as he
knew how, just what happened.

Because Thucydides was primarily a recorder of events, not
writing a systematic political philosophy, we must not look for
a simple statement of his beliefs, especially not by the favorite
amusement of quoting one sentence and ignoring the next; but

we search for the way his mind worked and so for some of his beliefs, as we may in Herodotos, in Gibbon or Macaulay, in Shakespeare or Milton, always bearing in mind that he still, for the most part, lets the story tell itself. It would be legitimate, however, to say of Shakespeare that we not only understand him, indirectly as it were, from *Macbeth*, but also directly in that he could create a character of such superb intelligence as Hamlet. So with Thucydides: that he could compose, or record, the Funeral Speech, shows that he appreciated the idea of democratic Athens that Perikles stood for and longed to instil into his fellow citizens. But we also know that, late in life at least, he could praise a drastic modification of the Athenian democracy as constituting the best government the city had known in his time.[3] Similarly, he understood what was meant by the daring and enterprise which Perikles praised in his countrymen (ii 41.4), and which they displayed under the command of Phormion, who used to remind his sailors that there was no superiority in numbers that they should not face (ii 88.2), and Nikostratos, or the equally remarkable daring of the Spartan Brasidas. Observe that this appears both in speeches and in the narrative of events; yet he not only understood also the different qualities of the normal Spartan, the unhurried steadiness, the enduring power of resistance (again shown both in speech, i 83–84, and in event, as the fighting on Sphakteria, iv 33–35, or at Mantineia, v 66–67), but praised the timid caution of Chios, which did not venture to secede from Athens till all seemed safe, because, he says, though prosperous, the Chians did not let success go to their heads, in this like the Spartans

---

[3] viii 97.2. This is the translation generally accepted; but it is not certain whether Thucydides meant that this was the best *form* of government Athens had had, or only that the city was then best administered. The connection with the previous sentence and τὸν πρῶτον χρόνον ("the first months of the new regime") suggest the latter ("many assemblies were held and sensible measures were taken"), but the following words μετρία γὰρ ἥ τε ἐς τοὺς ὀλίγους καὶ τοὺς πολλοὺς ξύγκρασις ἐγένετο may indicate that the *form* of government is meant. I incline to the view that "best administered" is right, and that μετρία ξύγκρασις refers to joint efforts by oligarchs and democrats (or, eupatrids and the masses), party feeling being laid aside; but I have kept the usual interpretation in the text.

and unlike, so often and so fatally, the Athenians, and, as we are of course tempted to add, unlike Croesus and Xerxes in Herodotos, and Xerxes and Agamemnon in Aeschylus.

Some, therefore, have concluded that this is all of Thucydides' thought, that he could only repeat a "lesson" learned from the older generation, "do not be rash, or overconfident"; they have forgotten Brasidas, not only his deeds which went to the very limit of rashness, but his words in encouraging much smaller cities than Chios to break with Athens and strike for freedom (Akanthos, iv 87.6, τοῖς τε Ἕλλησι ἄρξαι πρῶτοι ἐλευθερίας καὶ ἀίδιον δόξαν καταθέσθαι, "to start the liberation of Greece and win imperishable glory"; Skione, iv 120.3, οἵτινες . . . οὐκ ἀνέμειναν ἀτολμίᾳ ἀνάγκην σφίσι προσγενέσθαι περὶ τοῦ φανερῶς οἰκείου ἀγαθοῦ, "who had not timidly waited to be *compelled* to their own obvious good"). Take another passage, a well-known passage, from the last speech of Perikles when he is trying to rouse the Athenians from the weakness and lethargy which had so come over them during the pestilence that they were even asking the enemy for peace (ii 62, 3–5): "go to meet your enemies not only with pride in your heart, but despising them. Not boasting; that is for the fool in a time of prosperity or even for the coward. But to despise is the privilege of those whose *judgment* reveals that they are the stronger, which is our case now. Intelligence based on a feeling of superiority gives strength to daring; it does not rely on hope, which is the resort of the desperate, but on judgment based on true facts." Just Thucydides' own opinions? Elsewhere this paradox, that it is right to despise your enemies, does not appear;[4] on the contrary, it is recognized for the folly that it is (v 6.3; v 9.3–4). "Hope, the resort of the desperate": how often has this been quoted, and another from the speech of Diodotos arguing against rigorous punishment of Mytilene as a rebellious city: "it is hope that leads men to venture . . . no state has been stayed from war or individual from crime by fear of defeat or punishment, for all expect to survive. Hope and passion it is that do most harm, passion

---

[4] Except, it seems, in v 8.3, a very difficult sentence.

leading and devising the plan, hope following and suggesting the abundant generosity of fortune. For fortune does in fact often give victory to the weaker side." (iii 45.5–6.) But in another context another Athenian, also intelligent, caught in a very difficult situation, urges his men not to calculate, not to use their judgment (for to look around at the dangers on all sides, to calculate their chances, would make them fearful), but to rely on hope (iv 10.1); and optimism is a valuable quality in Athenians (i 70.3), and was occasionally, in exceptional circumstances, to be found even at Sparta (viii 2.4).

Even more interesting is the use elsewhere of Perikles' phrase γνώμη ἀπὸ τῶν ὑπαρχόντων, "judgment based on the facts"; what could be better? A cool head and a good brain will make daring something to be relied on. But the Spartans found that, just as good fortune will unexpectedly help the weaker, so even judgment based on the facts may prove wrong, may stumble; it failed them at Sphakteria (iv 18.2). Thucydides is constantly reminding us, not directly, but as usual by letting words speak for themselves, that the same words, representing the same thoughts, may in effect have different meanings when expressed either by different persons (as when Kleon and Alkibiades adopt but pervert the language of Perikles in defense of Athenian imperialism),[5] or in different situations. The importance of these fine distinctions between apparent similarities in the language of Perikles, Kleon, and Alkibiades, has often been noticed; another case, in its way of equal interest, is that of Archidamos and Brasidas, the former when threatening Plataia with immediate war: θεοὶ ὅσοι γῆν τὴν Πλαταιίδα ἔχετε καὶ ἥρωες, ξυνίστορές ἐστε ὅτι οὔτε τὴν ἀρχὴν ἀδίκως . . . ἐπὶ γῆν τήνδε ἤλθομεν . . . οὔτε νῦν, ἤν τι ποιῶμεν, ἀδικήσομεν· προκαλεσάμενοι γὰρ πολλὰ καὶ εἰκότα οὐ τυγχάνομεν (ii 74.2), and Brasidas in encouraging Akanthos to liberate herself or take the consequences: εἰ δ' ἐμοῦ ταῦτα προϊσχομένου ἀδύνατοι μὲν φήσετε εἶναι . . . , μάρτυρας μὲν θεοὺς καὶ ἥρως τοὺς ἐγχωρίους ποιήσομαι ὡς ἐπ' ἀγαθῷ ἥκων οὐ πείθω, γῆν δὲ τὴν

---

[5] See my article in *JHS* LXXI (1951), pp. 75, 78.

ὑμετέραν δῃῶν πειράσομαι βιάζεσθαι, καὶ οὐκ ἀδικεῖν ἔτι νομιῶ (iv 87.2).

The saying, however, that "even right judgment may fail," does represent one of Thucydides' constant and most profound thoughts: that men must, of course, form sound judgments, that one statesman is better than another because he has more foresight (πρόνοια), but for all that the event, particularly in war, is unpredictable. I quoted in the preceding chapter a wise statement of Winston Churchill's; he has given us another, which is a lot for one man: "It is not given to statesmen to see far ahead" (from his *Life of Marlborough*). So too thought Thucydides. He gives to Perikles a bold expression, "events can go forward just as stupidly, ignorantly (ἀμαθῶς), as the plans of men; that is why we blame fortune when anything turns out contrary to our calculations" (i 140.1). War, as it were, ignorant of how men have planned that it shall turn out, goes its own way.[6] (Incidentally, those who think that, because characters in Thucydides use picturesque phrases such as this one, and "fortune standing at a man's side" [παρισταμένη, iii 45.6], he therefore believed in fortune, not indeed as a god, but as a kind of impersonal spirit, something very primitive indeed, have forgotten this and similar sentences, as, e.g., iv 18.5; 64.1, μηδὲ μωρίᾳ φιλονικῶν ἡγεῖσθαι τῆς τε οἰκείας γνώμης ὁμοίως αὐτοκράτωρ εἶναι καὶ ἧς οὐκ ἄρχω τύχης, which is Shakespeare's "our thoughts are ours, their ends none of our own.") "Neither the justice of your cause nor confidence in your strength will guarantee success" (iv 62.4). Such a belief does not lead to despair; on the contrary, if we know that our best plans may not be realized, that they may indeed be upset by unforeseeable disaster, that we can never be sure of success, we shall be the less inclined, not only to rash undertakings, but to give way to misfortune (ii

---

[6] See Finley, pp. 313–315. Beaujon, pp. 97–98, speaking of the wrath of Achilles, says: "Il y a plusieurs phases de la colère. La première espèce de printemps de la violence, est la plus voluptueuse et la plus riche en liberté. Inspirés par le ressentiment, les actes se produisent à la manière d'une végétation tenace dont l'odeur se porte à la tête. Si, dans la suite, l'amertume prédomine, c'est que l'homme est prisonnier de la situation nouvelle, c'est qu'il doit faire la guerre après l'avoir déclarée. Elle lui impose sa loi."

64.1–2). Thucydides himself had failed at Amphipolis, and this gave him a sense of what failure meant.

It is expressions of this kind which make it impossible for me to agree with those who think that Thucydides had a cyclical view of history, that he was a determinist and believed that history repeats itself. He was not so simple. He thought that the same kind of events would happen again, for human nature remains the same; and so they have done, in the next century in the eastern Mediterranean, and in the twentieth century A.D. throughout most of the world. He has proved a truer prophet for our own time than he would ever have believed possible; that is why he makes now so direct an appeal, why he gets under our skin. Sometimes in my arrogant way I think that no one should deal with present-day international politics who has not studied Thucydides, and when I say "studied" I include every detail of language and history; sometimes in reverse I think that the gods arranged the flow of events in the first half of this century expressly so that we may understand Thucydides and the ancient Greek world. But to say that he believed that similar events would recur is not to say that he believed that events go round in cycles, still less that he thought they were in consequence predictable by anyone sensible enough to read his *History of the Peloponnesian War* (if, I suppose, he were living, and knew that he was living, at the right point in the cycle).

Nor was Thucydides a determinist in any other sense; to say, with Jaeger, that he was and that he was therefore unaware of the moral issue, because he said that "the growth of Athenian power *compelled* (ἀναγκάσαι) Sparta to go to war" (i 23.6), is to argue inattention to the rest of the book, particularly those two long paragraphs in which Thucydides forsakes his usual manner and speaks so gravely in his own person about the effects of civil strife. If one needs another example to show that he can use ἀνάγκη as we can use "necessity" without being a determinist, there is that in Brasidas' speech at Akanthos which I quoted just now in a different context (Akanthos, the city which he has come to liberate from the tyranny of Athens, the proclaimed object of the whole war), when near the close he says that, if they refuse to be liberated, then "I call on the gods and heroes of your land to witness that I am come for your good and you reject me, and I shall do my best to force you to be free by laying waste your fields. I refuse to think that I shall be doing wrong; *two necessities* justify me: first, Sparta's need; she cannot afford to let you go on paying tribute to Athens; and, secondly, that of Greece; her liberation from servitude must not be hindered by you." That should be plain enough. Both Greek and English words for "necessity," "the inevitable," are, philosophically, ambiguous. It is as legitimate to say that Athens had grown so strong that war was "inevitable," or that, being what she was, not only in character but by her situation as a sea power, she was certain to attempt the conquest of Sicily,[7] as it is to say that Achilles in the *Iliad* was bound to reject the first offer of reconciliation from Agamemnon.

A last point. It is said that whereas for Herodotos all human action and suffering begins and ends with the gods, for Thucydides everything belongs to man. "Hérodote fait tout venir des dieux, tout retourner à eux. L'homme qui s'est élevé trop haut est abattu par leur jalousie. Un Athénien, qui a vu pratiquer l'ostracisme, qui écrit lui-même à l'exil, a reconnu cette jalousie dans le cœur des hommes" (Thibaudet p. 127). This contrast between the two historians is, I think, too sharply drawn; as we have seen, for Herodotos the activity of the gods, and of the fate which was above even the gods, was not incompatible with human freedom and responsibility. But what I would emphasize again is that in both historians the generalization is not just superstitious, or superstitious in Herodotos and rational in Thucydides, but rational in both, that is, the result of observation, and where they accepted from their predecessors

---

[7] Thibaudet, pp. 92 and 122–123, commenting on Alkibiades' οὐκ ἔστιν ἡμῖν ταμιεύεσθαι ἐς ὅσον βουλόμεθα ἄρχειν (vi 18.3), "we cannot by careful husbandry fix the exact point at which our empire should stop," draws an interesting parallel with the naval power of Great Britain up to 1920. One point is especially interesting: "a naval power, Athens or Britain, must control all islands—India strategically is an island." Cf. the way Athens thought of Poteidaia, Mende, and Skione (iv 120.3, 121.2, 122.5).

and their contemporaries it was a rational acceptance. Observation showed that prosperity, apparently without a flaw, was
a slippery thing, and might suddenly fall, and that prosperity
and power together were especially dangerous. We cannot explain this, says Herodotos; I accept the view that the gods often
intervene in human affairs. Thucydides apparently did not
attempt explanation, and he certainly ignores the gods. (I
imagine Perikles' δαιμόνια [ii 64.2] to be intended as a concession
to his audience.) In this the two historians are a long way from
each other and in neither perhaps is the observation sufficient
or the reasoning persuasive, but it is inductive reasoning, nevertheless, from observed facts to generality.[8]

The impartiality of Thucydides has been much praised, and
not always understood. He is impartial between persons (with
the exception that the story of Kleon's death is biased, and he
draws perhaps too roseate a picture of Brasidas), between parties, and, almost as a matter of course, between his own city,
Athens, and her enemies. It is in this last aspect that I have my
one difference with Thibaudet, and it is worth while to examine
what he says. It is not accidental, he writes (pp. 47–48), that
the four surviving Greek historians, Herodotos, Thucydides,
Xenophon, and Polybios "sont des déracinés, des errants et des
exilés. Tous les quatre occupent la même position au seuil de
deux mondes, l'Orient et la Grèce, Athènes et Sparte, la Grèce
et Rome. La muse des destinées grecques paraît interdire au
citoyen de faire œuvre historique à l'intérieur et au service de

---

[8] It may be that I have not understood the implications of Dodds' second chapter in
The Greeks and the Irrational, but it seems to me that in his eloquent comment (p. 49)
on the chorus of *Antigone*, 583 ff., he has not sufficiently emphasized that, in part at
least, Sophokles is giving expression to the opinion (which is surely "right opinion,"
"true," based on observation, neither archaic nor modern) that men cannot command
success, neither saint nor sinner, as Solon said, neither the cunning sinner (Aristotle's
"clever but wicked man who fails," *Poetics* 56a22) nor the man stricken with a mad
hubris like Herodotos' Kambyses, who had his brother killed in an effort at self-
preservation, all to no purpose (iii 65). And hence success or failure is not the criterion
of conduct, as Phokion and Demosthenes knew and expressed so well (see pp. 175, 178),
and as so many Greeks recognized. That is why their victory over Persia astonished as
well as elated them, and why it was not surprising to them that they were defeated by
Philip.

la cité. La pure vie historique semble exiger alors le déracine-
ment comme la pure vie philosophique exigeait le célibat. Un
Thucydide se fût peut-être astreint à écrire pour le service de sa
patrie, mais il l'eût fait avec le remords d'un Archimède abais-
sant, sous l'empire de la nécessité, la science à des inventions
de machines à la défense de Syracuse." That is nice writing, and
Thibaudet speaks elsewhere of that peace of mind, that quiet
coolness ("la tranquillité de l'âme," "le sang-froid tranquille,"
pp. 43, 126), which Thucydides won by his exile, and which,
together with a family tradition, gave him his impartiality ("sa
facile impartialité historique," i.e., between Athens and Sparta,
"continue une tradition de sa famille," from the days of Kimon).
But there is in that view, I am convinced, a profound error.
Three of these four historians were indeed technically exiles,
forced to live away from their own cities, but none in any valid
sense was a wanderer, and only one of them, Polybios, was uprooted, and he alone stood on the threshold between two worlds.
Greece and Rome were indeed two, and Polybios knew that; it
was his great merit as a historian that he understood what the
sudden rise of Rome to the supremacy in the Mediterranean was
to mean. But Herodotos, though he traveled, was never uprooted, but at home in Greece; nor on a threshold between the
Orient and Greece, but comprehending both in his theme, and
understanding that the Greek victory meant not a new world
as the Roman victory did, but, mercifully, a continuance of the
old, Greece and the East existing side by side. Nor was Thucydides uprooted. Bitterly as he felt his banishment, because,
besides cutting him off from Athens (from Athens, the home of
wisdom and learning, πρυτανεῖον τῆς σοφίας), it ended suddenly
his active career—*he had failed*. How often must he have felt as
he watched the mistakes of his country, "if only I had been
present, I might have done something to help": ἐν τούτῳ κεκωλῦ-
σθαι ἐδόκει ἑκάστῳ τὰ πράγματα ᾧ μή τις αὐτὸς παρέσται. Yet he was
not in a foreign world. Athens and the Peloponnese were not two
worlds, but parts of one. Of Xenophon it might perhaps be said
that for him Sparta and Athens were different worlds between

which he was in some degree lost; but then, he was not impartial, and intellectually he was a little man. Of Herodotos and Thucydides it is as wrong to say they had lost their roots as it would be of Erasmus or Grotius or Buchanan in the Europe of the Renaissance, because they left for long years the lands of their birth. Europe was then intellectually one to a greater degree than it has been since, and the man of learning (and not he only) was at home everywhere; and it is one of the paradoxes of Greek history that, politically subdivided as they were, and jealous as each *polis* was of its independence (its right to have its own laws, its own currency and calendar, and its own dialect), and fight though they so often did with one another, yet all felt that Greece was one, with a common religion, common language, common customs and thought, so much so that there was no need for its frequent expression.[9] The poet, the philosopher, the artist, the historian would naturally go from city to city and expect to feel at home anywhere in the Greek world, without being, in the modern sense, a cosmopolitan. (It is characteristic that perhaps the only occasion on which Herodotos indulges in fine writing is in the two speeches which he assigns the Athenians in answer to the Persian proposals for a separate peace, to Alexandros of Macedon, the intermediary, and to the nervous Spartans: "The common blood and faith of Greece forbids" [viii 143-144]; and it is self-conscious and a little off the true. There is a further paradox, that Sokrates, who at least heralded the freeing of the individual's mind from all dependence on the community of which he was a member, was the one intellectual of Athens who would have felt uprooted had he left the Athens that he knew.) Thucydides was not a cosmopolitan, far from it, but he was writing for a Greek, not an

---

[9] *Repub.* v 469-470 is one of the best known of such expressions. (It is wrong to say that Plato here joins Isokrates in *recommending* a joint war against the foreigner. What he does is, primarily, to deprecate war between Greek cities as civil war, *stasis*, the word for war being properly reserved for conflict with foreigners, and to advocate mitigations of the customs of war in any *stasis* that arises. It is noteworthy that when Glaukon twice implies that war with the foreigner may be desirable, Sokrates passes the suggestion by in silence: *Repub.* v, 469c, 471B.)

Athenian audience, and composing a Greek, not a local history; his impartiality between the combatants had nothing to do with his family connections, but was expected, not remarkable, strange as this may appear to us for whom a History of England, or of France, or of the United States, is not felt to be local history, whereas for the Greeks a history of Athens was.[10] I do not mean by that that Thucydides, any more than Herodotos or anyone else, was completely impartial; he was, as I have already noted, biased against Kleon, inclined (I am coming to believe) to overpraise Brasidas—only that his impartiality toward his country's enemies was demanded of him by his profession of history.[11]

Thucydides, as I read him, was far from enjoying tranquillity of mind. His was a passionate nature, and one of his passions was for self-control, another was for the truth. Many have noted the impartial way in which he tells the story of the one campaign in which he played a leading part as commander of an Athenian squadron in Thrace, which ended in disastrous defeat; for this, technically at least, he was in part responsible. It is not only that he attempts no self-defense, to explain or explain away the failure; that would be quite foreign to his method, for in general he avoids individual biography and would eschew auto-biography most of all. It is that he does not exaggerate the importance of the campaign in which he took part, does not create "a grandeur even in defeat." Of what other general can we say, amongst the many that have written memoirs of their cam-

---

[10] Jacoby too, in his *Atthis*, misses this truth, as Thibaudet does. See my review in *CR* LXV (1951), pp. 84–85.

[11] Cornford, *Unwritten Philosophy*, p. 54, though writing from a different point of view (the divorce of the thinker from political life), is also, I think, misleading: "After Pericles, the men of thought, like Thucydides and Euripides, go into exile, voluntary or enforced. Socrates just fulfills his civic duties, but obeys the warning of the divine sign to keep out of politics." Surely men of Euripides' temperament had always kept out of politics; and we do not say that Aeschylus *just* fulfilled his civic duties. Neither Thucydides nor Plato, nor even Sokrates, lost his *interest* in the politics of the Greek state; the author of the *Republic* can hardly be said to appear to us "in his retreat at the Academy as completely detached from all that went on in the Assembly and the market-place as if the garden of the Academy had been the garden of Epicurus."

paigns, that he saw his own in proper proportion to others in a big war? Thucydides could obviously have told us so much more of the Amphipolis campaign than he has; but had he done so, it would have thrown the narrative out of scale. In no other part of his work is his passion for the truth, as he saw it, so clearly shown; he is impartial, not particularly to his victorious enemy or, what is less common, to his colleague in the command (who, it would seem, must have been quite incompetent), though he is that too, but, so to speak, to himself and his work as a historian. If we wish to discuss Thucydides' responsibility for the loss of Amphipolis, there is one argument that we must not use, that of the German historian Oncken, which is quoted with approval by Busolt (iii 1154, n. 4): "Thucydides' sparing use of words prevents us indeed from having strict proof either of his innocence or his guilt; but the silence of the accused is one of the many indications of his guilt." No; *Thucydides'* silence has a quite different meaning. But this passion for the truth (and here I come back to my main theme throughout this book)—is that the passion of the scientist, that he must observe and state the truth, or of the artist, that his work should be well-proportioned? I do not believe that in a historian these two things can be separated. But as artist at least, Thucydides shares this quality with all of his countrymen worthy of the name. The Greeks were obstinate, foolish, and cruel enough in their poli tics, greedy of power, fierce; at best "helping their friends and doing harm to their enemies," just like other civilized peoples; but in their art—put a pen into their hands or a brush or a chisel, and they do not know what partiality means; here at least they hardly took a step wrong. In this world of art there is no wicked enemy, no contest between white and black; the Trojans are not wicked in Homer, nor is Helen, nor the Persians and Egyptians, the βάρβαροι, in Aeschylus, the contemporary, who also, like Thucydides, had taken part in the events, or in Herodotos, nor the Spartans or some particular Athenian faction in Thucydides, nor in Aristophanes. Aristophanes is a good

case; men have admired the freedom with which he represented
his fellow countrymen in his comedies, and have marveled at
the pleasure they took in it, and the license, which was truly
remarkable, allowed him in wartime; but his impartiality is not
a political, but an artistic merit. Politics was often the theme
for his art, so that he must be impartial in that too, and if you
want a sympathetic picture of the waspish dicasts who formed
the support of Kleon, go to his arch-enemy Aristophanes (as
Plato, it is said, recommended men to do). Plato himself is an
even better witness; he was no lover of democracy in theory or
of democratic politics in practice, but his mocking description
of the democrats in the *Republic* is by far more understanding
than is his picture of the oligarchs or of tyrants, and praise of
Athens, as eloquent as that of Perikles in the Funeral Speech,
is to be found also on Sokrates' lips in *Kriton*, and not of Athens
as a center of "culture" (Sokrates was no sentimentalist), but
of her laws and their administration, by which he had himself
been condemned. Plato wrote *Kriton* not long after Sokrates'
death. With this in mind we can more easily understand how
Thucydides could compose the Funeral Speech, that eloquent
description of what Athens should be—her citizens making and
obeying their own laws, each respectful of the rights of others,
using thought, λογισμός, before coming to a decision, and other
like things: the same people who, incited doubtless by Kleon,
decreed his own banishment.

It is the same in the visual arts. In the beginning of the fifth
century men were thinking of the wars of the gods and the
giants, Lapiths and Centaurs, Greeks and Amazons, and the
Trojan War itself, as symbolizing the struggle of law and order
against chaos, civilization against barbarism. With some arrogance, if you will, they joined the Persian Wars with the legendary group; they themselves represented law, order, humanity,
light fighting against darkness. But in all the many sculptured
and painted representations of these fights we never see one side
heroic and the other mean or devil-like, nor any *victory* of the

civilized; but equal combat.[12] The artists knew who won and who should win if right was to prevail, but their instinct for avoiding the naïve contest between black and white prevailed. The Greeks did not *exult* in their victories; the defeat of their enemies was an example of general law, a law to both poet and historian, for all mankind; indeed they were always inclined to attribute it to their adversary's mistakes rather than to their own skill or courage. The Athenians may have "tyrannized" over their subject allies; they certainly gloried in their power and openly claimed their right to rule; the Parthenon was built in the heyday of the empire, partly with money contributed by those allies, but you do not see on its frieze one giant figure, whether the goddess Athena or a mortal, receiving tribute from a row of humble, suppliant subjects, but Athenians taking part in an Athenian festival, "in a kind of festivity," as Beazley said, many years ago, "which is at once a high religious ceremony and a delight to the participant. . . . It is interesting," he goes on, "to compare these men and boys and maidens and horses with the long line of tribute-bearers on the reliefs of oriental palaces or with the rulers of Rome in the *Ara Pacis Augustae*. In the union of common aims and individual freedom, in an order that never breaks down although constantly looking as though it would, the frieze of the Parthenon is a perfect illustration of that ideal of democracy which is expressed in the funeral speech of Pericles."[13] There is indeed no parallel in Greece to those fine friezes of Egypt and the East which commemorate the victories of mighty princes, which represent one kind of peace and order, subjection to the powerful. But in Athens—"an order that never breaks down, although constantly looking as though it would": how fine a description that is if we remember that it is of an ideal, a hope; in reality order did sometimes break down. That is what the *artist* represents, not an Athenian empire over others.

---

[12] So P. de La Coste-Messelière on the Siphnian frieze at Delphi of Greeks and Trojans; *BCH* LXVIII–LXIX (1944–1945), pp. 5–35.

[13] In *CAH* V, pp. 440–441.

VIII

The Fourth Century—Conclusion

IT HAD BEEN my original intention to say something about Xenophon; but I have spent my time in more important fields. Indeed, to begin with, when I first thought out the subjects of these lectures, I had fancied that I should, in the conventional manner, include Polybios in the survey; he had, like Herodotos and Thucydides, that necessary equipment for a historian, an understanding of his theme, not only its magnitude but its meaning—in his case, that the spread of Roman dominion meant both political union and the unification of Mediterranean history. He might almost have been thinking of that passage in the *Poetics* about the battles of Salamis and Himera, that they had nothing to do with each other, that it was fortuitous that they were fought on the same day; henceforth, he said, all events in the Mediterranean *will* form part of one story. Also, though he was not at all impartial between the Greek states, between his own and those that were its enemies, he was impartial between Greece and Rome, which for his history was the essential thing. It would, therefore, have been proper to include Polybios and to stay one's hand there, in that he relates what was to be the end of independent Greek history for many centuries; but I soon realized that it would not be possible without such compression of what I had to say about earlier writers as to make that material much less intelligible than I hope it has been. Even as it is, I must now abbreviate, and I shall, therefore, confine myself in this concluding chapter to one aspect only of fourth-century history and its records, and to a general conclusion.

There is a familiar story about Alexander the Great and Kallisthenes. The latter, a nephew of Aristotle and conscious of the value of his connection with the great man but not at all prepared to follow in his footsteps by hard work, erudition, and scientific principle, was accompanying the king as a kind of court historian; he would not mind writing a history of the great campaigns that would be light and readable. Alexander said to him, "Do you realize, Kallisthenes, how fortunate you are to have my deeds to record?" Kallisthenes replied, "Do you realize, Alexander, how fortunate you are to have me to record them?" It is a stock witticism and illustrates an ever-present problem: without Perikles, Brasidas, and the others, what would Thucydides have had worthy of record, as Plutarch inquires (*de glor. Ath.* 1, 345CD), and what would the world have known of Perikles and Brasidas had Thucydides not written, or, again, how far is Sokrates a *creation* of Plato? With this in mind we might make one of those easy parodies of well-known sayings and say that every period has the historians it deserves, and ask of fourth-century Greece, up to the victory of Philip of Macedon: "What more do you expect than the second-rate Xenophon, the flat and childish Ephoros, and the learned, shallow, rhetorical Theopompos, and that the works of these last two should not survive?" I am not, however, among those who regard a century which produced Plato, Aristotle, and Demosthenes, and ended with Menander, as one of decline, about which we must be apologetic. It is more pertinent to ask what does its history mean, and what have we by way of record.

There are scholars who see in the history of Greece (the political history) a long struggle for unity, an attempt to end the small-state particularism, a struggle temporarily won in the Persian Wars when at least some states joined forces for a common purpose, lost again when the leading Greek cities entered on a conflict which ended only with the exhaustion of the Peloponnesian War, and again in the more desolate wars of the first half of the fourth century when Sparta was predominant and had to be pulled down: wars which had less dignity than the earlier ones, for at least Athens had had some claim to empire, whereas Sparta, which had been good at leading equals, had no gift whatever for ruling—or is it only that Xenophon, not Thucydides, tells the story? Then, we read, the struggle for unity is won by the victory of Philip of Macedon. Among these scholars some at least have the good sense to see in the Athenian empire of the fifth century an attempt at unity; but others, who praise Philip and Rome, condemn Athens for using force, and declare that she failed for that reason, not seeing that the true cause of the failure was that the attempt came too late when the Greek political system, the small-state system, was already mature.[1] Others read the story of Greece differently, as that of a political system which by sheer good fortune came into being, but which was so difficult to preserve that, though it survived one great attack from without, it might at any time have succumbed to quarrels from within, and finally fell not by Philip's victory at Chaironeia, which was not the end of things (the Greeks had suffered defeat before and knew what it meant), but by what foolish sentimentalists like Isokrates had spent so many words in advocating, the Greek conquest of the East under the leadership of Alexander and his successors. We now sit comfortably back in our chairs, assert that the day of the small Greek state was obviously over, and censure the myopic glance of Demosthenes and Aristotle; and indeed there were ominous signs some time before Chaironeia, when men of action, able men, loyal to their city, yet found the city too small for them as such men had not done in the fifth century, and went away as soldiers of fortune and administrators to the services

---

[1] Fichte wrote: "How can the conception of one nation (from among the many small German states) arise at all? (Nor was Greece ever united. What prevented it? Answer: The single state prematurely grown solid.)" *Werke*, VII, p. 549, as quoted by L. B. Namier, *Avenues of History* (London, 1952), p. 22. Yet we can hardly blame those who condemn Athens while approving of Philip, for they learn from Thucydides and Aristophanes, Sokrates and Plato. The Athenians were so critical of themselves.

J. H. Finley, pp. 291–292 (followed by A. Maddalena in his edition of Thucydides i [Florence, 1951–1952]), maintains that Thucydides himself realized that in his day Greece had already passed from the small state system to one of larger unities, that material progress was impossible without them and that "the effort to achieve such a wider unity would provoke wars." I do not think he can be explained so simply as that. Material progress plays a prominent part in the earliest section of the *archaeologia*, but hardly any in the narrative of the war.

of Eastern princes. The spectacular achievements of Alexander dwarf, of course, the small quarrels of the Greek states; yet it was in the world of the independent Greek states, not in that of Alexander, that Western civilization was born and flourished, including, among many other things, the science and art of history, and it was the civilization of the small states that Alexander was to spread. The idea of the common brotherhood of man, fostered perhaps by his policy, might have compensated much for the loss of Greek political activities, but we shall never know whether the idea would have come to fruition or turned into a common servitude to one ruler ("I will apparel them all in one livery, that they may agree like brothers, and worship me their lord"); we must bear in mind how comprehensive and how tolerant of difference the Persian Empire had been, which was Alexander's predecessor. For after his death the single empire was divided into warring kingdoms, very large, each of them, by Greek standards, whose quarrels ended forever the chances of survival of the city-state system. There was no unity and no peace under the Successors. It was not till a century and a half had passed that these were at last won, imposed on the Greek world by Roman arms. And what a price had been paid; for Roman arms were quite unable to restore the creative vitality of the Greeks, which does seem to have required for its fostering the Greek political system with all its obvious disadvantages. That system had been for four hundred years before Alexander the Great in fact a triumphant success, a political success, but its survival all that time is as paradoxical as the military success it achieved over Persia.

We have Xenophon for the history of the fourth century down to the battle of Mantineia in 362, when the domination of the rapacious Spartans was finally ended, not only in Greece as a whole but in their own Peloponnese. But, as Xenophon observes with unusual sagacity, there was then greater confusion than ever. A great wrong had been put right by the victorious Thebans: Messenia, for three hundred years crushed under the Spartan heel, had been liberated, but the righting of a wrong, as so often, only created new problems, and there was no one to solve them. With all her faults, and they were many, Sparta had been a stabilizing influence for a long time and a center around which others would rally; men were used to her and now nothing was put in her place. She became a second-class power among other second-class powers. This was what the victors had wanted; they thought that they were doing good, but one result was that Sparta was absent from the field of Chaironeia twenty-four years later, and her presence there might have made as much difference as it did in the badly handled battle of Plataia against the Persians in 479. In Sparta's place were the Thebans who had been on the wrong side in 480–479, wrong because it was unsuccessful as well as because they had chosen it only to save their skins, and now at Chaironeia they fought the bravest and suffered the most, and their sufferings were largely due to their own misuse of the victory over Sparta. They had thought that it was their duty to punish wrong when they should have been thinking of what was politically wise and feasible, just as Thucydides makes Diodotos put it in the debate on Mytilene. They had supposed that they had established a new order by merely overthrowing the old, because they thought that they could see far ahead; yet they might have learned that particular lesson by their experience after the defeat of Athens in 404. Then, in the moment of victory, they were all for outright *punishment* of the tyrant city: "treat her as she deserves and destroy her." Within a year or so they were helping Athenian democrats to overthrow the regime set up by Sparta, and within ten years they and Athens were allies. You observe the dramatic irony of Theban history; I have not invented it, and I have not got it from an ancient historian who could not distinguish between drama and history. It is inherent in the events.

Athens was the only major state that was on the right side on both occasions, in success and defeat. She had made a remarkable recovery after the Peloponnesian War in most discouraging circumstances. The corrupt and incompetent democracy of the last years of the war—or so it is depicted for us, chiefly by

Xenophon who did not understand things very well, and by Plato who understood but, besides personally disliking the demagogic leaders, had an impossibly high standard of judgment—this democracy, after the defeat, was replaced by the government of the Thirty, supported by a Peloponnesian army of occupation. Some of these Thirty were relatives of Plato, and friends, who had been pupils of Sokrates, or at least well acquainted with him, and it is Plato who tells us that their conduct was such that the previous democracy seemed by comparison a golden age. He mentions one crime in particular which they attempted; they ordered Sokrates to act as their agent in arresting a man for execution against whom no charge could be brought; they coveted his money and wished to involve Sokrates. It is true that it is mentioned not as the worst crime committed by the Thirty, but primarily because it concerned Sokrates and his courage in ignoring the order; but if that was the opposite of what the corrupt democracy had done, well, it illustrates not only Plato's but the ordinary citizen's standard of political conduct. This tyranny of the Thirty was overthrown by a gallant band of democrats, helped by a political quarrel in Sparta that persuaded one party there to adopt a moderate and wise policy toward Athens. The restored democracy behaved with singular and determined moderation, restraining recrimination and revenge, though there were so many crimes to punish, so many wrongs to set right; they remembered that every punishment inflicted would but create another problem.

Plato once more, as when his friends were in power, though he was no friend to democracy, thought of entering public life; but it was soon all stained for him, and in consequence for us, by the trial and condemnation of Sokrates, and Plato returned to philosophy and letters.

When I considered this [he relates in the Seventh Letter, written nearly forty years later when he was growing old], and the men who were directing public affairs, and made a closer study, as I grew older, of law and custom, the harder it seemed to me to govern a state rightly. . . . It was not easy to find any associates to work with, now that Athens was no longer ruled by the manners and institutions of our fathers. . . . At the same time the whole fabric of law and order was going from bad to worse at an alarming rate. The result was that I, who had been at first full of eagerness to take part in public life, when I saw all this happening and everything going to pieces, fell at last into bewilderment.

(325c, Cornford's translation)

Cornford comments on this: "The whole tone of this letter reveals—what we might guess from his other writings—that his powers and gifts were of such a kind that he could never be a leading man of action in the society of his time. The plane on which his mind habitually moved was not one from which he could make effective contact with the plane of life in a demoralized society."[2] With all respect both to Plato and to Cornford, this is a misleading picture both of Athens and of Plato's mind. It suggests that "the Athens of our fathers," of Miltiades and Themistokles or of Perikles, was not going from bad to worse, and that Plato would have felt free to enter politics in their day. But we know what Plato thought of Perikles; he filled the city with docks and arsenals and material goods instead of with righteousness and justice. No need to say that he could not fit into politics "in a demoralized society"; he would not have fitted anywhere; his standards were different, his mind worked on a different plane. And we are entitled to point out that he founded his Academy in the Athens where "everything was going to pieces." There is in fact little evidence that democratic politics in Athens in the fourth century were worse than in the fifth. The quarrels and jealousies were not more deplorable or more laughable; Themistokles, Perikles, Alkibiades, would have found themselves at home. But there was one difference: the endless self-criticism, questioning, and mockery, had made them less confident than Aeschylus and Herodotos had been; they no longer felt that democracy was secure against decay; and Plato despaired when Heaven did not follow Hell, both when

---

[2] *Plato's Commonwealth* in *The Unwritten Philosophy* (1950), p. 52.

the Thirty succeeded the discredited democracy, and when democracy, restored, succeeded the Thirty. The Athenians were not only less optimistic, but more mature and more critical, less ready to be deceived, especially into a warlike policy; they were aware that the issue of a war is seldom as even the victors planned it. They were therefore more ready for peace, which so often means only peace and quiet, the purely negative ἀπραγμοσύνη. Philip won by his vigor and efficiency, and it is proper to demand vigor and efficiency from all who would help to defend a cause, whether with deeds or with words. Athens, the leader of Greece in 338 and again in 322, did not have quite enough: not enough prestige to win the rest of Greece into active alliance, and just not enough energy and ability to win with the few allies that she had. Yet the difference in the military *results* of the wars with the Persians and with Philip was due to this: both Darius and Xerxes by and large "fell by their own mistakes," as the Greeks themselves said;[3] Philip did not make mistakes.

To this it is worth while, I think, to add Plato's picture of a contemporary democracy, taken mainly from Athens, one may feel sure (*Repub.* vi 487c–488e). He has just stated that no single reforms will help at all, but philosophers must govern, and he is meeting the objection that in practice philosophers have not been very good at politics, but have been "a decidedly queer lot," if not worse, and the best of them useless. He takes the familiar simile of the ship of state; again I make use of Cornford's translation:

Imagine this state of affairs on board a ship. The master [that is, the owner who in Greek fashion is sailing with his ship, corresponding in the state to Demos, the people themselves] is bigger and burlier than any of the sailors, but a little deaf and shortsighted and also deficient in seamanship. The sailors are quarreling over the control of the helm; each thinks he ought to be the captain, though he has never learned navigation and cannot point to any teacher under whom he has served his apprenticeship; what is more, they assert that navigation is a

---

[3] E.g., Thuc. i 69.5.

thing that cannot be taught at all, and are ready to tear in pieces anyone who says it can. Meanwhile they besiege the master himself, begging him urgently to entrust them with the helm; and sometimes, when others have been successful in gaining his ear, they kill them or throw them overboard, and, after somehow stupefying the worthy master with strong drink or an opiate, take control of the ship, make free with its stores, and turn the voyage, as might be expected of such a crew, into a drunken carousal. Besides all this, they cry up as a skilled navigator and most knowledgeable captain anyone clever enough to lend a hand in persuading or forcing the master to set them in command. Every other kind of man they condemn as useless. They do not understand that the genuine navigator can only make himself fit to command a ship by studying the seasons of the year, sky, stars, and winds, and all that belongs to his craft; and they have no idea that, along with the science of navigation, it is possible for him to gain, by instruction or practice, the skill to keep control of the helm whether some of them like it or not. If a ship were managed in this way, would not those on board be likely to call the true navigator a mere stargazer, who spent his time in idle talk and was no use to them?

That is a good picture, and Demosthenes confirms its truth for contemporary Athens, so long as we remember that it fits fifth-century Athens, and any modern democracy, just as well. History, said F. W. Maitland, involves comparison; we must make sure, when we condemn a society as rotten or degenerate, that we mean what we say of that society compared with others.

For the political history of Greece in this period we have then Xenophon, which means very little, till 362, and for the important hundred years after 362 no history at all. In that century of years the first quarter was occupied by the struggle with Philip, and the last three quarters made it clear, what could not possibly have been clear before, that Philip's victory, and Alexander's over the Persian Empire, had after all been decisive. For that no history is extant; we have some later work which was based ultimately on contemporary, or nearly contemporary, historians, and we have Plutarch, who preserves so much, but who did not profess to write history and who lived

at a time when understanding of the small Greek states, especially of democratic politics, was impossible; but no history. We
have some documents for history, many official ones recorded
on stone, fragments of documentary evidence pitiably inadequate, from which however so much has been won by the skill,
industry, and imagination of modern historians, particularly of
course in America. Besides official documents the writings of
Plato and Aristotle and their successors are evidence, but when
we speak of the documentary evidence of this period, we are
thinking chiefly of Demosthenes—of his speeches, and a few
others of contemporary politicians. In a way these take the
place, not of a history, but of the political comedy of Aristophanes. Neither speech nor comedy can do the work of history; the light they throw on their times is too vivid, pinpointed
to particular events and leaving much in shadow, directed also
from very peculiar angles. Aristophanes was a poet and a man
of genius, and you may demand much from him; but Demosthenes? A politician and not a philosophical one; not very successful, not very wise, not generous, one would say; at best one
of those empirical politicians whom Plato describes as having
no knowledge of principles but only a knack of "divining what
might happen next" (*Repub.* vii 516CD). If only, one is tempted
to exclaim, politicians had as much knack as that! (Plato, we
may remind ourselves, was thinking of the fifth-century giants,
Themistokles and Perikles, each famous for his foresight, the
former τῶν μελλόντων ἐπὶ πλεῖστον τοῦ γενησομένου ἄριστος
εἰκαστής, says the *historian* in praise: Thucydides i 138.3.)
What can Demosthenes' speeches contribute except a few details, and these of doubtful truth, about particular events, since
we are, in the absence of a history, in the dark about the events
as a whole, partly indeed dazzled by the light he throws on this
or that detail? The speeches in Thucydides' history, however
authentic their matter, present a more philosophical, a general
picture—a search for the truth "dans son être et son résultat,
et non dans son devenir et son progrès, sa durée et sa vie," as
Thibaudet puts it (pp. 62–64); but those of Demosthenes,

though edited doubtless for publication, we yet see very much "in their coming into being, in their life," belonging to the particular occasion when they were delivered—that meeting of the Athenian assembly,—urging a particular policy, the sending of an army or a fleet here, or an embassy there, in the mortal struggle with Philip. These surely can only be scattered documents; we have only about twenty of his public speeches and another thirty to forty which belong to the law courts, some of which deal directly with public affairs. But no. Demosthenes was sincere, and had a divine gift of style that, like the poetry of Hómer, "sinks deep into the recesses of the soul." His speeches are documents—so is Thucydides' history a record of particular things which happened,—but what documents! For the understanding of the period, the nature of the struggle between Athens and Macedon, what the forces on either side were (the general weaknesses of government by discussion against such an able autocrat as Philip, and of the Athenian democracy in particular—all so well known to the Athenians, and to us from them, not from their enemies; and yet how near Demosthenes' *words* came to defeating the redoubtable army of Philip), and what failure meant: for all that and for the Athenian refusal to sacrifice their own system, that is, what they were fighting for, in a foolish attempt to imitate the efficiency of their enemy, Demosthenes, the demagogue, the envious politician, gives what is required. By instinct rather than by foresight he proved a true prophet that failure would mean the end of those fortunate circumstances in which the Greek world had come into being and had continued to live; in fighting for the city-state he was fighting for all Greece as Aeschylus, Herodotos and Thucydides, and Plato, had known it and wished it to be. And he said something more, namely, that defeat did not prove that his policy had been wrong; it was the only policy that was worthy of Athens and her traditions, as he says more than once, and most eloquently, after the defeat, in the great passage in the *Speech on the Crown* where Goodwin paused in his comment on the details of language and history to say that he did not

envy the man who was strong enough to read it without emo-
tion. Demosthenes is the true heir to Perikles in the *History* of
Thucydides. His countrymen must act according to their high
standards, and success is no criterion of conduct; indeed all
things mortal must decline, but you may leave behind you an
imperishable name. Rather better, is it not, and wiser too than
the grave modern historian who only says that what happened
had to happen; the day of the city-state was over and Demosthenes was stupid not to see it. We say that he was calling upon
his Athenians to behave as though they were the Athenians of
Perikles' day; but was the conduct of the latter much better?
True, there was nothing heroic about the Athenian fighting at
Chaironeia; they fought bravely enough, but only as other men
do. It was no Thermopylai, nor did the defeat inspire song. But
then, very few peoples have fought their last battles very
heroically. This is history, not romance. These men of the
Athens that we love seem indeed to have been born only for
the sunshine,

> χαίρετε, χαίρετ' ἐν αἰσιμίαισι πλούτου·
> χαίρετ', ἀστικὸς λεώς,
> Παρθένου φίλας φίλοι,

to live always

> ὄφρα μὲν ἠὼς ἦν καὶ ἀέξετο ἱερὸν ἦμαρ[4]—

the men so resilient, so active in mind and body, as they had
been described by their enemies in Thucydides ("never quiet
themselves and never letting others live in quiet"), or by their
own leaders as "so good at being deceived by novelty and so
reluctant to follow what has been proved to be sound, slaves of
every paradox, condemners of what is usual, every one of whom
would like if possible himself to be an orator, and, failing that,
to rival the speakers in speed of following the argument and
applauding a clever saying before it has been uttered, as quick

---

[4] Beazley in *CAH* V, pp. 441–442. Ἐν αἰσιμίαισι πλούτου corresponds to Herodotos'
τοῦ βίου εὖ ἥκοντι ὡς τὰ παρ' ἡμῖν on Solon's lips in speaking to the fabulously wealthy
Croesus (i 30.4). How grave is the splendor of Aeschylus by comparison.

to forestall what was said as they were slow to foresee its consequences, looking for things other than those amongst which we live" (Thuc. i 70.9, iii 38.5–6). In Aristophanes "quick to make up their minds, and quick to change them again" (*Acharnians* 630–632), or Demos, "a little old man, fed on voting-beans, quick-tempered, rustic-minded, hard of hearing," deceived by his flatterers and flattering himself that he knew all about that, with his bitter sting for those who, for the moment, had fallen from grace, yet one who loved the old songs of Phrynichos and had no patience with the newfangled (*Equit.* 41–43, 1141–1150; *Vesp.* 266–280). In Plato, the city with such a passion for variety, freedom, and equality that even domestic animals catch the prevailing spirit, the "horses and donkeys walking down the street with all the dignity of free men, running into anyone they meet who does not get out of their way"; where "you are not obliged to be in authority, however competent you may be, or to submit to authority if you do not like it; you need not fight when your fellow citizens are at war, or remain at peace when they do, unless you want peace; and though you may have no legal right to sit on juries, you will do so all the same if the fancy takes you. . . .

There is a charm, too, in the forgiving spirit shown by some who have been sentenced by the courts. In a democracy you must have seen how men condemned to death or exile stay on and go about in public, and no one takes any more notice than he would of a spirit that walked invisible. There is so much tolerance and superiority to petty considerations; such a contempt for all those fine principles we laid down in founding our commonwealth, as when we said that only a very exceptional nature could turn out a good man if he had not played as a child among things of beauty and given himself only to creditable pursuits.[5] A democracy tramples all such notions under foot; with a magnificent indifference to the sort of life a man has led before he enters politics, it will promote to honour anyone who merely calls himself the people's friend" (*Repub.* 557–558, Cornford's translation).

---

[5] See above (pp. 57–58) the quotation from *Rep.* 400–401, and contrast with this Perikles' claim in Thucydides ii 37–38.

All that *requires*, does it not, the sunshine? Yet these are the people who also, remarkably, knew the lesson of failure. Phokion, contemporary with Demosthenes, but an honest soldier with no love for politicians and with a defeatist attitude toward the ever-active Demosthenes, knew it too; in recommending acceptance of peace after Chaironeia he bade the Athenians remember that they had known both victory and defeat in the past, and had served Greece well in both. There are not many people who have been eloquent in just this way.

The defeat of Athens is history, not romance; it is also not poetry. We come back to our original inquiry into Aristotle's distinction between poetry and history, and ask ourselves whether we can make any useful statement about it. When Aristotle said that the poet's theme was how a certain kind of person would act, and the historian's how a particular person (or state, one should add) did act and suffer, he was stating an important truth, for that is why we have different criteria for poetry and for history, why we ask of Herodotos questions about his account of the Persian Wars that would be quite irrelevant if asked of Aeschylus,—and not only, did things happen just in this way, but is his interpretation of the events *correct?* When Homer describes the bay of Phorkys in Ithake, we do not bother because just such a bay is not, in fact, to be found there, for there might so easily have been one, but when Thucydides says that the island of Sphakteria was fifteen stades long instead of twenty-five, it is proper to point out the mistake. Both Homer and Thucydides imply that there are no special obstacles in the journey from Pylos to Sparta, but only in the historian does this matter. But Aristotle's statement that poetry deals with the universal, history *only* with the particular, and therefore poetry is more philosophical and of graver import, is a very different matter. His belief or his apparent belief that historians can only chronicle *all* events within a period has also, clearly, some truth in it; we criticize, for example, Thucydides for not mentioning the big increase in the tribute assessments of

the cities in the Athenian empire which was made in the middle
of the first ten years' war; but when we do, we mean that it is
logically connected with the story, not merely that it was an
event within his period. We should not criticize Herodotos had
he omitted all reference to the battle of Himera, if we think
that it had, logically, nothing to do with the Persian Wars.
Further, we are concerned with something much more important than the problem of inclusion or exclusion of events within
a period, or even of events proper to the theme of a *History*,
namely, with the manner in which events are narrated, that is,
with the question whether it is not also written καθόλου, generically, equally with poetry, if in a different way.

Consider it in this way. We should all agree that we are not
interested in what Achilles actually did (that is, the historical
Achilles who is behind the character in the *Iliad*) and whether
the quarrel had the results which Homer says it had, *except as
Homer compels us*, for Achilles and Agamemnon are, for us, his
creation. Are we much affected by the behavior of Athenian
jury courts in the 420's B.C.? We are, but only because Aristophanes makes us. Homer and Aristophanes were both poets
and therefore wrote generically, and that explains it; but what
of Xerxes? Is it only Aeschylus who compels our interest?
Clearly not; Herodotos does too; in a different way, because he
was a man of different temperament, but to an equal degree.
But that is only because he wrote in the epic, or the dramatic
manner, that is, as we should say, unhistorically? Unhistorically as Cornford, for example, thought when he wrote of Thucydides' criticism of Herodotos: "he accuses him of trivial
errors, and does not bring the one sweeping and valid indictment which is perfectly relevant to his own point about the
embellishment of the Persian War. The dramatic construction
of Herodotus' work, which stares a modern reader in the face,
apparently escaped the observation of his severest ancient
critic" (*Thucydides Mythistoricus*, p. 135); and it is abundantly
clear that Aristotle too in the *Poetics* when his purpose *is*

literary criticism, as that of Thucydides was not,[6] quite failed to see Herodotos' dramatic construction. It is, you observe, an indictment.

I will not repeat why I disagree with this judgment as it affects Herodotos. It will be easier to answer it if we turn to Thucydides, for we find that he compels our interest in these long-past wars, not only in the speeches which in some special way might be described as "poetic" in Aristotle's sense and "written generically," but in his narration of events—the pestilence, Athenian victories at sea, the deeds of Brasidas, the destruction of Mykalessos, the fighting at Syracuse. It will be yet easier perhaps if we turn to Demosthenes; we are not now *stirred* by the question whether the help sent by Athens to Olynthos will be too little and too late, unless we read the speeches. Then we are; yet, as I said, what could be more local and particular than a speech delivered to urge a particular policy at a particular meeting of the Athenian assembly? The answer must be that if you are eloquent enough, as Demosthenes was, you lift the question from the particular to the general, without ceasing to be the advocate, the earnest advocate, of that policy; and if a man writes history well enough, as Thucydides did, his narrative has all the power of poetry to compel our interest because it is written "generically" without ceasing to be an exact record of particular events, of what Greece, all Greece, "did and suffered" in the Peloponnesian War; that is, the generality, as in poetry, is embodied in particular instances. If something new is found about Athens in Thucydides' day, fragments of an inscription giving us an official statement about some action, or of a contemporary comedy with some *scandale* about her politicians, scholars are at once

---

[6] In any case, his criticism of Herodotos was not for "embellishing" the account of the Persian Wars, in the sense of making them "bigger" or more important than they really were. (Doubtless he did not believe Herodotos' figures for the army of Xerxes, but these figures are not what constitute τὸ μυθῶδες in Thucydides' mind or "the dramatic" in Cornford's; they are a sign only of inaccurate information and of misunderstanding of military movements.) Nor was Thucydides Herodotos' "severest ancient critic."

busy with it, piecing the parts together, fitting them to something else that we know, or think we know, about her, and this for two reasons, not for one only: partly because this work is to be done for its own sake, to discover facts, professional scholarship having its own value; but also, and to a greater degree, because we are interested in *Thucydides'* Athenians as we are interested in Homer's Achilles.

"Truth," said Davenant,[7] "narrative, and past, is the idol of the historians, who worship a dead thing; and Truth operative, and by her effects continually alive, is the mistress of Poets, who hath not her existence in matter but in reason." But Herodotos and Thucydides are not dead. This is after all what we mean by saying a work is a *classic*, that it does not belong only to its own time and place; and in this sense Herodotos' and Thucydides' *Histories* are as "philosophical" as Homer's epic or the plays of Aeschylus and Sophokles. There too there is "the ability to see in particular human experience," if not "some significant symbolism of man's general destiny," as Lascelles Abercrombie said of epic (above, p. 28), something at least that is other than the facts themselves, that is a significant picture of human conduct and destiny.

---

[7] Preface to *Gondibert*, quoted by Prickard in his essay on the *Poetics*.

Index

INDEX

Ancient Authors Cited

GENERAL